Organized Crime: A Very Short Introduction

VERY SHORT INTRODUCTIONS are for anyone wanting a stimulating and accessible way into a new subject. They are written by experts, and have been translated into more than 45 different languages.

The series began in 1995, and now covers a wide variety of topics in every discipline. The VSI library currently contains over 550 volumes—a Very Short Introduction to everything from Psychology and Philosophy of Science to American History and Relativity—and continues to grow in every subject area.

A Very Short Introduction available now:

Available soon:

For more information visit our website

www.oup.com/vsi/

Georgios A. Antonopoulos and
Georgios Papanicolaou

ORGANIZED CRIME

A Very Short Introduction

OXFORD
UNIVERSITY PRESS

OXFORD

UNIVERSITY PRESS

Great Clarendon Street, Oxford, OX2 6DP,
United Kingdom

Oxford University Press is a department of the University of Oxford.
It furthers the University's objective of excellence in research, scholarship,
and education by publishing worldwide. Oxford is a registered trade mark of
Oxford University Press in the UK and in certain other countries

First edition published in 2018

Impression: 1

Published in the United States of America by Oxford University Press
198 Madison Avenue, New York, NY 10016, United States of America

British Library Cataloguing in Publication Data
Data available

Library of Congress Control Number: 2017955742

ISBN 978-0-19-879554-4

Printed in Great Britain by
Ashford Colour Press Ltd, Gosport, Hampshire

Contents

List of illustrations

Chapter 1
What is organized crime?

Stories and images of organized crime are impossible to miss today. Policymakers, law enforcement, and the media rarely fail to bring up the issue when discussing the nature and seriousness of contemporary criminal threats, and the appropriate responses towards them. For many people around the world, instances of what is described as organized crime may be part of their everyday experience in their neighbourhoods, their streets, the places they work and live. Many more are familiar with the notion of organized crime: from *Godfather* and *Scarface* to *Pulp Fiction*, *The Sopranos*, and *Breaking Bad*, the film and TV industry regularly draw on fictional or real figures and situations to fascinate audiences with violence and intrigue unfolding in an obscure underworld. Organized crime feels like a tangible, inescapable issue in today's world.

The problem is, the more 'organized crime' is the topic of public debates and popular culture, the more it feels to many like a known and well-defined reality. The very label 'organized crime' defies even the elementary intellectual defences an average consumer of stories, proclamations, explanations, and images is likely to raise. To be sure, 'organized' suggests association and collaboration, but what kind of people, and how many people are involved? Is 'organized' meant to evoke the image, the operations, and the power of a legitimate organization, such as a corporation?

Are the people involved as well-coordinated as in a corporation? To what particular ends? Can any type of crime be organized, or are there particular crimes that the label 'organized crime' applies to? What is the scale of the criminal activity? And, does this activity differ between countries? What happens when it extends beyond borders?—Well, 'it's organized crime'!

This short book does not pretend to offer definitive answers to all these questions. Rather, what we aim to do is help readers navigate their way through an ocean of information. Ambivalence and conflicting approaches and viewpoints do not pervade public representations of organized crime only. In the United States, where the idea began, an early consensus about what organized crime was soon gave way to intensive debates among those who studied the phenomenon. As organized crime became an issue for policy in other countries, the debates about its definition became wider and more divisive. Similarly, there has been a variety of legislative and policy approaches across different countries, according to how the issue is perceived in each. The development of cooperation between states against organized crime depends on consensus around a legal definition. The United Nations and the European Union have taken very broad approaches, essentially relying on the 'minimum common denominator' characteristics of organized crime.

It is safer to say that while, overall, there is some agreement about some characteristics of organized crime, there is no complete agreement, let alone one uncontested definition of it, whether scientific or legal. The root of this confusing state of affairs is found in the different perspectives of those who are in a position to shape how the various phenomena associated with the label 'organized crime' are understood in society. Crime, its causes, consequences, and efforts to suppress it, all represent a complex reality, which is understood by each one of us in society in different ways depending on our experiences, ideas, and values. Additionally, this understanding is shaped by powerful institutions and organizations that actively attempt to influence how an issue is viewed and addressed depending on their interests and aims. A similar divergence and diversity of views can be found among those who study organized crime, since their various theoretical backgrounds and methodological preferences, and the demands institutions make on scientific research are all likely reflected in their approaches.

The state of flux in which the concept of organized crime often seems to be found is also due to the fact that its development has been a policy and scientific endeavour that emerged in the second half of the 20th century—that is, fairly recently. The label 'organized crime', however, applies to illicit activities that have occurred regularly throughout history in various geographical contexts, and economic, social, and political conditions. Criminal activities such as piracy, banditry, smuggling, and the trade in illegal goods, the exploitation of labour under conditions of slavery, fraud, or extortion have long preceded the concept. Retrospectively, it is even possible to understand a wider variety of phenomena, such as the abuse of corporate power, speculation, or the bribery and corruption of officials, as historical instances of organized crime. The very early use of the words 'organized crime' was itself ambiguous as it applied to disparate phenomena ranging from political violence to conventional crime committed perhaps by more capable criminals.

The association of 'organized crime' with professional criminal groups, a stereotypical representation of the phenomenon in popular culture, particularly in connection with specific ethnic groups, has a distinctive United States origin. The social anxieties and the moral crusades against vice and crime during the Progressive Era paved the way, ironically, for an unprecedented growth in organized crime. The Progressives' preferred tools for social engineering—prohibitions, such as those on gambling, drugs, and, most famously, alcohol—opened up the opportunity for large-scale, highly lucrative underground enterprise. The Great

Prohibition is remembered as the time of unbridled bootlegging and racketeering, of gangster wars and the rise of some iconic mobster figures, such as Al Capone, 'Bugsy' Siegel, 'Lucky' Luciano, or Meyer Lansky. The formulation of the concept of organized crime carries the marks of the experiences of that period, involving strong and typically violent criminal groups, substantial illicit enterprise, and public corruption.

The diverse group of social scientists who study organized crime approach it by focusing on three different aspects, all of which were arguably visible in those early manifestations of the phenomenon. What makes organized crime different from conventional crime can, first, be the very element of the criminal collectivity. In other words, there is something particular about the way criminals associate or link with each other. Their association can be understood as something akin to organizations as we experience them in everyday life, a system of activity directed towards a common purpose, involving membership, rules, roles, and a work system to accomplish its goals. Criminal association can also be understood as a network, involving patterns of activity between participants who are connected more strongly or loosely and take up opportunities depending on their social position. Viewed as a network, these individuals do not necessarily commit themselves to a common purpose beyond their individual interests, preferences, and type of activity.

Second, organized crime is different from conventional crime because of the nature of the criminal activities it involves. Planning, preparation, complexity, and continuity over time are all characteristics that set organized crime apart from the spontaneous, perhaps ill-thought out transgressions involved in most everyday-life crime. An essential feature of organized crime, however, is that it involves the extraction of financial gain from the particular illicit activity, or range of illicit activities. Approached from this angle, organized crime can be understood fundamentally as criminal business, in which those involved take

4

up an opportunity to participate in an illicit market, by producing or supplying illicit goods or services. The smuggling of drugs and other goods, human trafficking, illegal gambling schemes, fraud schemes, or loansharking are examples of criminal businesses. In some cases, criminals create the market, by creating a demand and making an illicit gain for the 'services' they provide. This is, for example, the case when organized crime interferes with legitimate activity.

Third, organized crime can be understood as an accumulation and use of power that is akin to the power of a government. This understanding first addresses from an economic viewpoint the possibility that organized crime groups as producers or suppliers of illegal goods and services may seek to monopolize a market, as this would maximize profits. It may also happen that several criminal firms act in combination, forming a cartel, to monopolize a market. Such monopolistic aspiration is often linked to the possibility of violence, as a means to eliminate competition. The idea, however, that organized crime may mimic the functions of a government arises from the special condition that its activities unfold in a power vacuum. A legitimate government exercising control over territory, people, and their activity by definition aims to disrupt and suppress illicit activity that occurs against the rules it sets. However, the production and supply of illicit goods and services is still a social activity that creates a demand for setting rules and enforcing them, resolution of conflicts, and also protection from external threats. The Calabrian 'Ndrangheta is a prime example of an organized crime group performing such a quasi-governmental role.

Organizational, or network structure, illicit enterprise, and extra-legal governance provide entry points to an understanding of organized crime. One should not imagine that a combination of all three would provide a clear and useful definition of organized crime. Many students of organized crime often prefer to develop a list of characteristics of organized crime as a tool for understanding what it is, but items on such lists could be disputed depending on one's preferred entry point to the phenomenon. Historically, there has been an ebb and flow of such preferences, also depending on policy considerations or national contexts of the phenomenon. In the 1950s and 1960s, organized crime in the United States was strongly associated with a robust, hierarchical organizational structure, involving bosses, soldiers, and other roles. Identified with Italian American gangsters, 'the Mafia' or 'Cosa Nostra' came to represent organized crime par excellence, and was widely viewed as an underworld conspiracy and a grave threat to society. This view was subsequently challenged by scholars in the United States, and in other countries, particularly in Europe. In those contexts, illicit entrepreneurship existed in ways that did not resemble the narrow view of organized crime of the American Mafia.

The quest for conceptual clarity in the study of organized crime has been further complicated in the final stretch of the 20th century as a newly perceived threat, that of organized crime crossing borders, began its ascendancy to an agenda-topping issue. Major geopolitical changes, such as the collapse of the former Soviet bloc or the faster pace of European integration, and developments such the Internet and the informatization of the economy, as well as the increased cross-border mobility of both persons and goods, were not merely seen as facilitators and amplifiers of older cross-border flows of illicit goods and services. They also brought about an expansion of criminal opportunities across borders, by opening up new illicit markets, by allowing the exploitation of gaps and 'asymmetries' in legal frameworks and enforcement. Ultimately, they may have allowed new actors to get on a now global scene of organized crime. Transnational organized crime is sometimes understood as activity conducted on an international scale as organized crime structures establish a presence and perhaps control of criminal markets in new national contexts. A more likely image is that of transnational criminal networking, building on opportunities for criminals to meet and link up their business.

Another aspect of transnational organized crime relates to the weaker relevance of physical space and borders in a globalized world. Cyberspace, the borderless and often anonymous universe of digital communication networks, may facilitate the interaction and activity of criminal groups across borders. Importantly, it may be giving rise to new forms of criminal activity using digital technology, such as the trade in stolen data and virtual goods. Whether the concept of organized crime applies to these new forms of crime is a moot point: cybercrime often evokes a sense of organization and sophistication that may mislead one to assume the presence of 'organized crime' when, in fact, there is none. More generally, the idea of transnationalization captures the possibility and ease of traversing physical borders or cyberspace in a globalized world about crossing borders, but this does not mean that criminal groups are necessarily able to engage in it. Their structure, activity, and the ways they relate and interact with their social environment often depends on familial, friendship, or ethnic relations within their local context. This characteristic may represent a considerable barrier to their ability to scale up their presence or business across borders.

It will be clear at this point that formulating a definition or general framework to understand organized crime is an endeavour fraught with difficulties. While the dimensions of structure, activity, and extra-legal governance provide the general coordinates of the phenomenon, they are not themselves homogenous categories. The approach we are taking in the remainder of this book may further impress these difficulties on our readers. We believe that ultimately a bottom-up approach will be more informative. We discuss, first, a number of contexts in which organized crime structures exist around the world and relevant collectivities that have been associated with such structures. The nature, characteristics, links with the sphere of the 'upperworld' (legal businesses, law enforcement, politicians, the state, nationalist organizations, etc.) will be looked at, and some historical context that assists in their understanding will also be provided, where possible. Second, we discuss the types of business in which organized crime is involved. Although our discussion cannot possibly involve an exhaustive list of organized criminal activities, it covers a wide spectrum of possibilities in the reality of organized crime, from predatory activities (e.g. extortion) to illegal markets of legal commodities (e.g. tobacco) to illegal markets of illegal commodities (e.g. drugs) and so on. Third, we discuss the types of policy and law enforcement approaches intended to address organized crime as an issue. We will return to drawing a synthesis and comprehensive picture in the final chapter of this book.

Chapter 2
Organized crime structures around the globe

In Chapter 1, we stressed the idea that the various manifestations of organized crime and the context in which these can be found are important for understanding what organized crime is. In this chapter we take a look at how organized crime is manifested in different contexts around the world. Our discussion is selective because our aim is to illustrate primarily how different structures of organized crime exist in particular contexts. In other words, we wish to draw our readers' attention to how criminal organization and context are linked, rather than provide an inventory of organized crime by country or region.

The connection between organized crime structures and particular national or cultural contexts is appropriate as a first entry point because, traditionally, and often in popular culture, organized crime has been understood through the lens of ethnic links. The media, too, very often report organized crime with reference to the ethnic origin of criminal groups. A consideration of the organized crime structure in a particular national or cultural context will help readers reflect on the extent to which manifestations of organized crime are unique to that context or whether they could be relevant and even replicate themselves and proliferate in other countries too.

Italian and Italian-American organized crime

The Italian 'Mafia' is an obvious starting point because it provides the exemplar around which organized crime is constructed in the media and public perception. Often, separating reality from fiction is difficult because of the sensational and consistent representations of Italian and Italian-American organized crime. The Mafia has also proven to be a powerful template for policy, and for the study of organized crime. 'Mafia' is not, however, a uniform reality, and we begin by differentiating immediately between the situation in Italy and the Mafia phenomenon in the United States of America.

There are four sets of 'entities' that are generally referred to as 'Italian organized crime' by law enforcement agencies in Italy and the rest of the world. Especially since the 1990s, however, there are other small and flexible groups that operate in that country, often in close collaboration with non-Italian criminal groups. The four sets of entities we discuss are the most prominent ones, but they do not control every (organized) criminal activity in Italy or even their territory.

The establishment of the Sicilian Mafia first relates historically to the establishment of secret societies leading the fight against the various ethnicities invading and occupying the island of Sicily (the Greeks, the Vandals, the Arabs, the Bourbons, etc.). It also has its roots in the *gabellotti*, individuals who acted as mediators between landowners who lived in the cities and peasants in rural areas, and who were able to extort from both parties. In the 19th century, particularly after the unification of Italy and the transition to more modern economic and social structures, the new Italian state was unable to enforce property rights and establish its monopoly of the use of legitimate force. Alongside the *gabellotti*, a range of individuals and groups, many of which were simply armed Sicilian families, filled the governance gap.

The Sicilian Mafia is organized around a hierarchical structure called *cosca* ('group'; *cosche* in plural), and currently it is a confederation of approximately 150 groups. It has been suggested that the Sicilian Mafia supplied the 'model' for Italian-American organized crime.

The 'Ndrangheta originates from the region of Calabria at the southernmost part of the Italian peninsula. The term *'Ndrangheta* is rooted in the Greek work *andragathia* meaning 'manly virtue' or 'bravery'. Its origins date back to the unification of Italy, but it emerged as a particularly powerful actor in the 1990s, when the Sicilian Mafia became weaker and Calabrian clans started investing money from their local criminal activities into the much more lucrative drug trade. The 'Ndrangheta is organized around the *'ndrine* (singular: *'ndrina*) clans that are hierarchical, and are based on blood ties and kinship. This characteristic allows them to be insular, and exert significant influence over the locality they are based in.

The Camorra (*camorra* means 'quarrel') is based in Naples and the wider region of Campania. Since the 1950s, when impoverished rural populations, including groups who controlled agricultural markets, moved into Naples, the Camorra has predominantly been an urban phenomenon. It has very little in common with the Mafia groups that existed in Campania in the 19th century. Unlike the Sicilian Mafia and the 'Ndrangheta, the Camorra is not a confederation of groups, but a set of independent criminal groupings, some of which are family-based. Because of this lack of structure, violent confrontation between and among Camorra groups that strive for control is common.

Apulian organized crime is found in Puglia, the area in southeastern Italy around the cities of Bari, Brindisi, Lecce, and Foggia. The term mostly refers to the *Sacra Corona Unita* ('United Sacred Crown'), which emerged in the early 1980s when members of the Camorra and the 'Ndrangheta were imprisoned in correctional facilities in Puglia. Apulian organized crime also applies to criminal groups such as the Società Foggiana, the Camorra Barese, and Gargano's Mafia.

Italian Mafias, and especially the Sicilian Mafia and the Calabrian 'Ndranghera, share common cultural characteristics, such as an emphasis on family bonds and kinship, masculinity, loyalty, and reliance on the 'brotherhood', respect, and honour, as well as rituals and symbolisms. For instance, the initiation ceremony includes the index figure of the candidate being cut so that blood drips on a saint's small icon. The icon is then set on fire in the hand of the candidate, who declares loyalty to the Mafia and adherence to its rules. An important rule, among others, is the obligation of Mafia members not to disclose information about the structure, composition, activities, and plans of their group to outsiders or the authorities. This code of silence is known as *omertà*. These cultural norms have been used by Mafia groups as defence mechanisms to protect themselves from the authorities.

Perhaps the archetypical Mafia activity within Italy is protection, and, in fact, Mafias monopolize protection at the local level. According to the Italian authorities, in Sicily's capital, Palermo, approximately 80 per cent of the 100,000 businesses pay protection money (*pizzo*) to the Mafia. In some localities in southern Italy there has been a 3 per cent Mafia 'tax' on all commissioned construction works. Apulian organized crime groups have been extorting funeral parlours in Puglia. Italian Mafias are also involved in drug trafficking, human smuggling and trafficking, cigarette smuggling, stolen vehicles smuggling, products counterfeiting, illegal gambling, and loansharking.

Some Mafia groups, particularly 'Ndrangheta clans, have also used family ties throughout the country, as well as the communities of Italian emigrants in the United States, Canada, a number of European states, Australia, Latin America, South Africa, and elsewhere to expand their business. While Mafias have expanded their activities throughout Italy and abroad, they have always remained embedded in, and heavily dependent on, their territory of origin. While all Mafias tend to have diverse criminal and legal portfolios within Italy, different Mafias tend to favour specific activities abroad. For instance, 'Ndrangheta's main business internationally is the drug trade.

The Mafias have invested in a variety of cash-intensive sectors (e.g. tourism or catering) and real estate. They have been particularly skilful in infiltrating legitimate businesses and economic sectors. Occasionally they have achieved monopolies in southern Italy, and at the same time they have used these economic sectors to launder money from criminal activities. Camorra clans have been highly successful in gaining control of significant economic sectors in Campania, such as the waste management sector and garment manufacturing, often hidden behind legal companies. The 'Ndrangheta has almost monopolized the construction, real estate, and transport sectors in Calabria. By intimidating members of the local community, and with the assistance of corrupt politicians in the local administration, they have a grip on the bidding process for public works. Reportedly, the Italian Mafias invest heavily in alternative energy projects in Italy.

Mafia involvement in politics and infiltration of the Italian local and national politics have been integral features of Italian organized crime. Apart from the collusion or support of politicians, which sometimes has been facilitated by links with masonic lodges, the Sicilian Mafia and the 'Ndrangheta have strived for political control in their territories of origin. Along these lines, they could be seen as quasi-governmental structures that informally legislate, administer justice, settle disputes, and exert control on every economic production and decision-making process. A clear example of 'Ndrangheta systematically intersecting local public administration is the case of Reggio Calabria city council, which was dissolved for Mafia infiltration in 2012. The

Sicilian Mafia at a point significantly challenged the authorities. From the late 1970s onwards, and especially during the 'reign' of Salvatore 'Totò' Riina, the Sicilian Mafia assassinated politicians and members of the judiciary and the police. The assassinations of anti-Mafia prosecutors, Giovanni Falcone and Paolo Borsellino in Palermo in May 1992 and July 1992, respectively, are the best-known cases and caused a very strong reaction from Italian society and the state. Since the early 1990s, consistent anti-Mafia efforts by policymakers and law enforcement in Italy have led to significant blows to the Sicilian Mafia and to a lesser extent other Mafia groupings in the south of Italy. These efforts were considerably facilitated by confessions of the *pentiti*, former Mafia members turned state witnesses.

Italians were only one of the many immigrant groups in the US in the 19th century. Other groups, such as the Jewish and the Irish, were also perceived as the major 'threats' in relation to what could be described as 'organized crime' at that time. Interest in Italian organized crime emerged after the lynchings and shootings of Italian suspects that followed the killing of a New Orleans police chief in 1890. Interestingly, no connection between Italian organized criminals and this murder was ever proven. From the end of the 19th century onwards, Italian-American criminals were involved in illegal gambling, loansharking, counterfeiting, prostitution, as well as some legal industries, such as garbage disposal and construction. They were also involved in the extortion of Italian businessmen in schemes that would typically involve demanding money by threatening to bomb the business or kidnap the owner.

Italian-American organized crime grew, expanded, and perhaps consolidated its position during the Prohibition era in the 1920s. The 18th Amendment to the US Constitution and the ensuing Volstead Act of 1919 prohibited the manufacture, transportation, sale, or importation of alcohol within the United States from 1920 to 1933. Prohibition was important not only because it provided fertile ground for Italian-American organized crime to flourish and move beyond the enclaves of the local ethnic Italian communities. It also became the context in which many important figures such as Al Capone (Figure 1) in Chicago came to the forefront, and as a result it boosted a specific perception about the organization of the business, particularly in the media and in popular culture. The sense was that local gangs were joining powers in a centralized, large, and extremely powerful illegal entity with the aim to monopolize the alcohol business. 'Proof' for such development could be found in a three-day meeting in Atlantic City, described as the first summit of US crime bosses in May 1929.

In 1950 and 1951, Senator Estes Kefauver chaired the Senate Special Committee to Investigate Crime in Interstate Commerce, and raised the issue of organized crime in the United States.

1. Al Capone's bulletproof and bombproof Cadillac photographed in 1933.

According to the Kefauver hearings, there existed 'a sinister criminal organization known as the Mafia operating throughout the country…a direct descendant of a criminal organization of the same name originating in the island of Sicily'. Despite the absence of credible evidence, the law enforcement witnesses called by Kefauver laid the foundations for claims regarding a nationwide Italian conspiracy, according to which organized crime had been imported in the United States via Italian immigrants. A meeting of Italian organized crime figures at the home of Joseph Barbara in Apalachin in 1957 reinforced this impression of imported organized crime threatening American society and economy. Later, in 1963, an informant, Joseph Valachi, appeared before a US Senate Sub-Committee on Investigations (the McClellan Committee) and revealed the existence of *La Cosa Nostra* (meaning, 'our thing'). The latter originated from the Sicilian Mafia, although it eventually incorporated Italian crime groups of non-Sicilian origin. Valachi also described a feud between the major factions of Giuseppe Masseria and Salvatore Maranzano in 1931, the Castellammarese War. The 'war' resulted in sixty deaths and eventually led to the formation of the then 'new' Mafia in New York consisting in the Bonanno, the Colombo, the Genovese, the Gambino, and the Lucchese families. Each family was said to have a hierarchical structure with a boss (*don*) on top, beneath him an underboss (*sottocapo*), and a counsellor (*consigliere*), who advised the boss. These were followed by captains (*caporegimes*), who in turn controlled a number of soldiers (*soldati*) each. The families also involved 'associates', who worked for the family, but they were not members of it. Infamous gangsters of non-Italian background such as Bugsy Siegel and Mickey Cohen were associates of Italian crime families. The captains, soldiers, and associates formed the so called 'crews'. The bosses of the families were connected to one another through what has been known as the 'Commission', an informal arrangement for conflicts to be avoided, disputes to be resolved, and joint business endeavours to be decided and facilitated. The idea for the Commission was introduced by Lucky Luciano, one of the most important figures in the Italian-American organized crime scene especially in New York.

A more careful look at the Valachi testimony reveals that the families were not centralized to any significant extent, nor were the members of each family 'employees' of the family boss receiving orders. Instead, the 'crews' were semi-independent sets of criminal actors, who were involved in illegal markets and activities knowing that they had the permission, support, and protection of the family for a share of the profits made. Since the beginning of the 1970s, the FBI concentrated its efforts on the Italian-American community and found out numerous forms of collaborations that hinted towards criminal organizations. However, the FBI evidence also suggested that there was limited capacity and power of the 'Italian-American Mafia' to control illegal businesses and other criminal activities in specific localities and, of course, on a national level.

Irrespective of its structure, Italian-American organized crime has had an extremely diverse portfolio of activities. Beyond the activities mentioned earlier, Italian-American criminals have also been active in labour racketeering. They have been used to break strikes, to keep wages down by controlling the labour unions through violence and the threat of violence, to extort businessmen by threatening strikes, as well as to embezzle union health and benefits funds. Interestingly, perhaps, Italian-American organized crime has not been heavily involved in drug trafficking. An exceptional case in New York has been the so-called called the 'Pizza Connection', which involved the collaboration of Sicilian and Italian-American Mafias in importing and selling heroin through a chain of pizzerias between 1975 and 1984. It has also been suggested that Italian-American organized criminals have control of numerous cash-intensive businesses and have a grip on the construction industry and the waste disposal industry. Through the (often hidden) ownership of casinos in Las Vegas and Atlantic City, as well as infiltration in Wall Street stock market by controlling brokerage firms, they amass big profits and launder illicit proceeds.

Italian-American organized crime does not have the presence (or the political influence) that it used to have until the 1980s. The reasons for this decline have been the successful law enforcement efforts against it, and the increased competition by other ethnic groups. Currently, it tends to be concentrated in its 'traditional' hubs in the northeastern US such as New York, New Jersey, Boston, Chicago, and Philadelphia, where it still has some influence on the local administration.

British organized crime

Unlike Italy or the US, British organized crime has never really been described in terms of 'Mafia'. It has been an extremely diverse terrain, which shows clearly how political, social, and economic developments can shape and transform organized crime. The eras ranging from the medieval times all the way through to the industrial revolution and the great urbanization affected not only the types of crimes various collectives were involved in, but also resulted in new forms of 'organized crime'. For instance, in pre-industrial Britain, the maritime smuggling of excisable luxury commodities such as tobacco, brandy, tea, and coffee was commonplace, while the establishment and maintenance of British colonies largely depended on state sponsored pirates.

The industrial revolution affected road travel, resulting in a new breed of robbers, the so called 'highway robbers', who operated mostly in rural areas. At around the same time, and even more after the 1830s, professional criminals displaying elements of organization were involved in predatory street criminal activities including pickpocketing, shoplifting, and theft in inner city London and to a much lesser extent smaller urban centres. Such crime was, in fact, an integral part of Victorian Britain. The marketplace that emerged from the early years of British urbanization was crucial in the formation of organized crime, creating networks of poaching and smuggling that transcended the rural-urban divide, and which heavily depended on a division of labour. Economic organized criminal activities were also present. Various forms of frauds ranged from bankruptcy frauds, which were common from the late 1860s onwards, to fraudulent investment schemes as well as embezzlement that involved bank clerks working alongside highly respected London bankers.

In the 1920s, the Sabini brothers were prominent figures in the London 'underworld'. Their major activity and source of income was protection in racecourses and, later on, running nightclubs and illegal gambling dens. They were powerful enough to grant permission to groups of thieves or other criminals to operate in the West End of London. Other gangs with similar range of activities existed in London and also in major cities throughout Britain, such as the Cortesis, the 'Elephant and Gang Mob', and Billy Kimber and his 'Birmingham Boys'.

The 1930s saw notable figures of the British professional criminality such as self-proclaimed 'Kings of the British Underworld', Jack Spot and Billy Hill. These onetime allies turned enemies, had a reputation for being violent men in their own localities, and were involved in racecourse protection and protection of illegal drinking establishments. The framework for modern British organized crime was established during World War II. At that time, when the eyes of the world were on the battlefronts, the British underworld thrived by taking advantage of shortages of any kind. Groups of professional criminals, many of whom avoided military service, raided government offices for ration books, and counterfeiters produced fake clothing and petrol coupons in bulk. Other groups would steal and sell everyday commodities such as razor blades and cigarettes, whereas food and alcohol fraud with potentially immense consequences was rampant. Two examples of such activity come from a consignment of sausages in Hackney, London, containing tuberculous meat, and from the selling of industrial alcohol that could cause brain damage in West End clubs and bars. The profits from criminal businesses were so big for some that the infamous gangster 'Mad' Frankie Fraser reportedly said: 'The war years were the best years of my life. Paradise. I'll never forgive Hitler for losing the war.'

Criminals who were particularly successful during the war, including some of the violent men, continued their activities in the late 1940s and 1950s. These were a mixture of protection/extortion, selling alcohol, prostitution, and gambling. The major figures were in a way the predecessors for the Hollywood celebrated Kray twins (Box 1) in East London and the Richardson brothers in South London. Both sets of brothers depended on extended families, and they had a strong working-class neighbourhood base, which was crucial to their identities. In the 1960s, through a network of allegiances, they came to dominate other parts of London, too. They enforced an order though violence and the threat of violence. The Richardsons in particular became well known for their brutal torture methods, despite their general entrepreneurial attitude.

Although the Krays, who had assumed the status of national celebrities, and the Richardsons were well known to law enforcement and public alike, they were not the only groups involved in criminal activities in the 1960s. During the 1960s and 1970s, numerous criminal groups were involved in stealing commercial cash in safe-cracking and small business robbery schemes. These were typical activities of what has been called 'craft crime', the illegal parallel of 'apprenticeships' in the world of industrially organized labour. In the same way younger labourers were apprentices to more experienced labourers in various legal industries and trades, in the underworld younger criminals were 'apprenticed' to older and more experienced criminals. Innovations in security technology, which raised significant obstacles to criminals, and very importantly the decline

Box 1 The Kray twins

Identical twins, Reginald (Reggie) and Ronald (Ronnie) Kray were born in the East End of London on 24 October 1933. Their father deserted from the British Army in 1939 and rarely visited the family for about twelve years. The twins were effectively brought up by their mother, Violet. At a very young age Reggie and Ronnie established their own gang. Ronnie was more aggressive than Reggie and he was considered the dominant twin. Boxing was a passion for the twins and at the age of 17 they were known for their capacity for violence which extended beyond rings. Their father introduced Reggie and Ronnie to traditional London criminals who taught them the cultural code of the East End criminal including toughness, pride in one's fighting ability, smartness, and disregard for law and the authorities. Mentored by Billy Hill, the twins progressed in London's underworld. Their first business venture was, at the age of 21, a billiard hall. By 1960, the Krays were successful and known extortionists, and already making money. They gave the title 'The Firm' to their organization. At their peak they owned property, betting shops, restaurants, and respectable clubs in the West End of London, which attracted celebrities, famous artists, playboys, and politicians. Unlike the Richardsons, their South London rivals who owned a scrap metal business partly dealing in stolen metal and was used as a façade for other activities, the Krays did not keep a low profile. During their time, they mimicked the style of the classic screen gangsters, such as James Cagney, Humphrey Bogart, and George Raft. In 1966, Ronnie killed George Cornell, a Richardson organization member, at The Blind Beggar pub, a popular meeting place among London criminals; and, in 1967, Reggie killed Jack 'The Hat' McVitie for failing to perform a contract killing. The twins were eventually arrested for the murders, their trial lasted thirty-nine days and, on 4 March 1969, they sentenced to no fewer than thirty years in prison. Ronnie died on 17 March 1995 of a heart attack and Reggie on 1 October 2000 of bladder cancer.

of the cash economy, led to these activities being replaced by what can be described as 'project crime'. This depended on some specialist skills, precision, planning, and organization and very importantly the physical attributes that one was expected to find in industrial labour. Typical activities would include burgling or robbing banks and warehouses. Perhaps the most iconic case of this type of crime was the Great Train Robbery, which involved a group led by Bruce Reynolds robbing the Glasgow to London Royal Mail train of £2.5 million in 1963 (Figure 2). Generally, British organized crime from the 1930s to the 1970s, its 'Golden Era', was based largely on loyalty, and on masculine traits that were essential for working-class people in the industrial era (e.g. toughness, smartness, autonomy). It was embedded in the urban working-class environment with its practices, cultures, and emphasis on the locality.

By the 1980s, the new organized crime landscape was shaped by a new spirit of entrepreneurialism instilled in British society in the wider context of de-industrialization. De-industrialization led to the disintegration of working-class neighbourhoods and the local

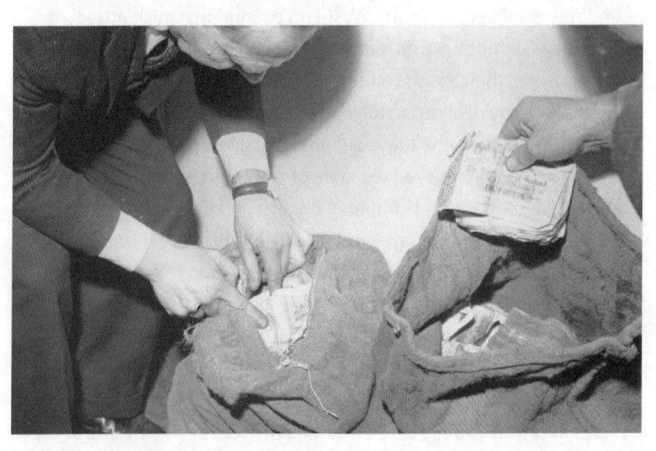

2. £2.6 million was stolen after a group of robbers held up an overnight Glasgow to London mail train.

labour markets that were the basis of the traditional (1930s–70s) criminal 'firm'. The new criminal landscape, reflecting the legal employment landscape and unpredictable economy, was now based on small, flexible, mutating, often ephemeral, and overlapping networks of entrepreneurs, who drifted from legal to illegal activities and back when opportunities were present. 'Traditional' activities, such as extortion, did not completely disappear, but largely became another business item in the diverse portfolios of groups involved in security in the night-time economy. Moreover, armed robberies were still possible, with the most well-known case being the Brink's-Mat warehouse robbery at London's Heathrow Airport. In that instance, six armed robbers escaped with £28 million worth of gold bullion in November 1983. Armed robberies, however, largely changed from a professional activity that required planning and impeccable execution into an amateur activity counting on improvisation.

The contemporary British criminal entrepreneurial environment is demand-driven, perhaps best exemplified by the drug trade. Since the 1980s, drug markets have been an inclusive field for a myriad flexible collectives and individuals. According to the British National Crime Agency (NCA), organized crime groups are also involved currently in the provision of legal and illegal commodities and services, acquisitive crime, human smuggling and trafficking, and economic crimes. British organized crime groups have maintained their local focus, and some still have a familial basis (e.g. the 'Adams family' in London; and the Sayers in Newcastle). Unlike their predecessors from the 1930s to the 1970s, they are more flexible, they cross ethnic and class barriers, and they also take up the international entrepreneurial opportunities offered to them by global markets, information and communication technologies, and international legitimate business networks. For example, in many tobacco smuggling cases, legitimate businessmen (e.g. international transport company owners, warehouse owners, etc.), who know one another from previous legitimate projects in the EU, invest funds in illegal tobacco importation schemes. In many cases, British criminals migrate to other countries for criminal business. Investigations by the Dutch police, for instance, reveal that British criminals have settled in the Netherlands to facilitate drugs transports, because of the position of Amsterdam in the international drugs market.

Russian organized crime

It has become commonplace to refer to Russian and post-Soviet organized crime as the Russian Mafia or *mafiya*, but this is a rather misleading term. First, many 'Russian' criminal groups involved, in fact, other ethnic groups, such as Chechens, Georgians, and the Uzbeks. Second, what is described as the Russian *mafiya* is not one organization, but a wide range of groups, whose structure, home base, power, reach, and even legality may vary significantly. There is no single Russian criminal organization controlling entire illegal markets in Russia or abroad, but, rather, overlapping, flexible networks with a wide range of actors including criminals, businesspeople, law enforcement agents, and politicians. It is very difficult to provide an accurate figure for the number of Russian organized crime groups operating in Russia or abroad. Some official estimates exist, such as those of the Russian Ministry of Internal Affairs (MDV). In the early 1990s, it was estimated that there were approximately 5,000 crime groups in Russia alone, with a total membership of approximately 100,000. These organized crime groups varied significantly in size, with the Solntsevskaya (originating from the Solntsevo district of Moscow) being the biggest.

Russian organized crime has a history that spans centuries. It is rooted, first, on independent groups of beggars or underworld professionals that were reported in Russia as early as the 15th century, known as *arteli* ('cooperatives' or 'guilds'). These cooperatives were present in Russian cities, and other cities across the former Soviet Union up to the 20th century. After the 1917 revolution, a crucial phase of the Russian underworld started with the phenomenon of the *vory-v-zakone* ('thieves-in-law'), a hierarchical community of criminals adhering to an old code of conduct for criminals. This community featured a dislike for legitimate work and the authorities, and forbade the *vory* from serving in the army, having a family, or having a permanent residence. Membership and the individual criminal history of a 'thief-in-law' was recorded on his or her tattoos. For example, an eight-pointed star on shoulders denoted a high-ranking 'thief'.

Between the 1950s and the 1980s, the social base of organized crime in Russia became wider and much more diverse, due to the presence of shadow economy entrepreneurs. These *tsekhoviks* collaborated with communist party members and other officials in a variety of illegal trades (caviar, cotton, currency, etc.) and accumulated significant amounts of wealth.

The widening of the social base of Russian organized crime was exacerbated in the post-Soviet 1990s with the coming of the 'violent entrepreneurs'. This was a diverse set of groups, including outrightly criminal groups, legal private protection companies, state police and security forces acting as private entrepreneurs, and other public authorities. The groups were established by and recruited among young sportsmen (wrestlers, boxers, weightlifters, etc.), Afghan war veterans, and members of the security forces, including the KGB. President Yeltsin's government reforms in the early 1990s, and the cutbacks in government funding for sports, resulted in large-scale unemployment among the former state security officers and sportsmen, and created huge pools for potential criminal group members.

These 'violent entrepreneurs' used organized violence to offer protection or extort legitimate and illegal businesses. Evidence from the 1990s suggests that small groups of thieves, robbers, and professional killers, with no hierarchical structure, also paid protection money to larger groups controlling the area in which they operated. 'Violent entrepreneurs' used violence to supervise contracts, settle disputes, and recover debts (since protection from the authorities was insufficient or non-existent), to negotiate with state organizations and help obtain permissions, registration, licenses, and tax exemptions as well as to incur damages and sabotage activities of competitor companies. Their efficiency was such that some of these entrepreneurs were hired by legal companies. For example, the leader of the Tagirianova group, who was an expert in shady financial schemes, was hired as financial manager by Gazprom, the state natural gas company, to 'facilitate' transactions.

In the context of privatization, important national companies, such as mineral and energy companies, were sold at an extremely low price in rigged tenders to some of the entrepreneurs, especially the ones that were politically well-connected. For instance, in 1998, the Tambovskaya group was reported to own the major share of the Petersburg Fuel Company, a prominent company in the refinement, storage, and retailing of oil and petrol in northwestern Russia. The so called 'oligarchs' emerged through the acquisition of profitable state companies for small amounts of money. These oligarchs now form part of the business elite, and exercise influence over the political elite. Based on a diverse and rich criminal tradition, the nature of contemporary Russian organized crime is the product of the political and economic transitions that took place in Russia during the 1990s. The transition blurred the boundaries between licit and illicit businesses and markets, and the government, official groups, and criminal groups even further, and consequently allowed criminal groups to infiltrate and be incorporated into legal businesses and the state.

Apart from protection and extortion, Russian organized crime groups have engaged in a variety of other activities, including kidnappings and contract killings, counterfeiting of official documents and goods, illegal gambling schemes, the trafficking of licit and illicit commodities such as agricultural products, cigarettes, oil, drugs, weapons, and nuclear material (facilitated by the selling of Russia's arsenal to high ranking army officers in the 1990s), car theft and trafficking, trafficking in human organs, trafficking of women for the sex industry, and various fraudulent schemes from credit card fraud to medical care fraud. Russian organized criminals have also been active in Internet-based crime. For instance, one of the most prolific counterfeit medicine traders online known to the authorities is the Russian-based GlavMed, which has been described as one of the most significant cases of organized cybercrime in the pharmaceutical sector. There have also been organized crime groups with political objectives. Perhaps the most known example is the Obshina group, which has been heavily involved in armed robberies, extortion, and the drug trade in order to fund the Chechen separatists. The activities of the Russian organized criminals are not limited only to Russia or the Commonwealth of Independent States, but can also be found in other areas with sizeable groups of ethnic Russians, in countries such as the United States and Israel as well as in several countries of Eastern and Western Europe, Australia, Japan, and South Africa.

In the 1990s, Russian organized criminals established their own banks to manage their finances and launder money from other illicit activities. It has been suggested that, in the latter half of that decade, crime groups controlled as much as 60–80 per cent of the Russian banking industry. This allowed them to become significant money laundering service providers. In the last ten to fifteen years, many groups have been laundering their money through mainstream banking in locations with appealing financial and tax infrastructures, such as the City of London. Other laundering schemes involve legal companies in Russia as well as the tourism sector and real estate in countries such as Cyprus, France (French Riviera), the UK, specifically, the London property market, and also Greece, Portugal, and Spain. In 2013, for example, the Spanish authorities arrested four Russian nationals suspected of laundering €56 million from the Solntsevskaya and the Solomonskaya groups through restaurants, gas stations, and real estate in Catalonia. These groups also had shell companies in Cyprus, the Seychelles, and the British Virgin Islands.

Turkish organized crime

Contemporary Turkish organized crime has deep historical roots. During the Ottoman Empire, the predecessor of the modern Turkish Republic, rebellious political and religious groups, the *kabadayi* (local 'urban knights'), who sold protection in urban neighbourhoods, settled disputes and were widely respected and feared, and groups of bandits, who operated in the mountains, were the historical building platforms of modern Turkish organized crime. After the collapse of the Ottoman Empire in 1923, a vacuum of power emerged as the early Turkish Republic was not in the position to fully enforce the law. Local underworld groups and individuals such as the *kabadayi* served as informal agents of social control. It was the *kabadayi* who evolved in a way into the heads of crime families that were highly active in international smuggling of heroin in the 1970s, before being reportedly incorporated in the Turkish so-called 'deep state'.

There has been a traditional, mutually beneficial relationship between organized crime and the authorities and state in Turkey. There have been, for instance, claims that large-scale drug trafficking would not have been possible without at least the tacit connivance of the Turkish state. Some reports move even further suggesting that after 1980 it was the Turkish army that controlled the heroin trade in Turkey. On the other hand, there have been claims that serious organized criminals along with ultra-nationalists have taken part in many of the secret actions of the 'deep state', such as those against Armenian nationalists and Kurdish separatists, who have also used the drug trade to fund their operations. Organized criminals have reportedly conducted covert operations under the orders and supervision of conveyors of the Turkish state ranging from arms trafficking to liquidations of political opponents. A car accident near the town of Susurluk in November 1996 highlighted the complex relationship between organized crime, ultra-nationalism, and the Turkish state. The passengers that were pulled out of a destroyed Mercedes included a police chief, an MP, a beauty queen, and Abdullah Çatli, a famous drug trafficker and contract killer, who was also recognized as the second-in-command of the ultra-nationalist group, the Grey Wolves.

There have been two types of Turkish organized crime structures. First, small, flexible criminal groups, which are based on village, town, or area of origin; relationships forged in prison; and political views. These groups are very often opportunistic and do not specialize in a specific market or activity, but on smuggling in general (*kaçakçilic*). They have a small membership, no hierarchical structure, and are open to collaboration with individuals with specific resources and skills within Turkey and in other countries. When it comes to international activities, these groups capitalize on political and religious ties to form collaborations. There are, for instance, collaborations that involve Turkish and Azerbaijani nationals.

Second, family-based crime groups, which are internationally known primarily because of their heavy involvement in the international heroin trafficking since the 1970s. They are reportedly responsible for more than 70 per cent of the heroin smuggled into several European countries each year. These groups have a major role as heroin wholesalers, and this is primarily because Turkey is the main opium processing country. Initially, opium is transported from Afghanistan and Iran to Turkish Kurdistan. Then the opium is transported to processing laboratories in Asia Minor (in the west) or Istanbul to be transformed into heroin. From there heroin is transported to the destination countries of Western Europe. The groups that are responsible for each part of the process (importation of opium, transportation of opium from east to west of Turkey and processing into heroin, and transportation to final markets) are independent cells that have control over a segment of the process only, and are connected with strong family/clan relationships. The presence of Turkish families in all crucial locations is a result of migration within Turkey and in various European countries such as Germany, Belgium, the Netherlands, France, and the United Kingdom since the 1960s and 1970s. These groups capitalize on the importance of family in Turkish society and culture. Structured like cells, they naturally follow the relationships among family members and the obedience to the head of the family, the *baba* (Turkish for 'father'). Members also include male individuals from the *baba*'s extended family, such as nephews, cousins, brothers-in-law, sons-in-law, etc. It should be noted however, that professionals, such as lawyers and accountants, should be considered parts of these 'families', even though they may not be connected by family ties in the strict sense. The home bases of the biggest Turkish family crime groups have been Istanbul, Ankara, Adana, and Mersin (in the south and close to the border with Syria), the cities of Samsun and Trabzon in the Black Sea region (coincidentally a hub of Turkish ultra-nationalism), as well as Diyarbakir (the unofficial capital of Turkish Kurdistan). It is interesting to note that Hüseyin Baybaşin, perhaps the most prominent figure of Turkish organized crime and also known as the 'Emperor', is of Kurdish background. On some occasions, two or three families have worked together in a scheme and it has been reported that links and trust between families have been forged through marriages.

Since the 1990s, the family-based groups adapted to the new drug-related entrepreneurial environment, including the declining heroin market, by becoming more versatile in the types of drugs they deal. They are now involved in the cocaine, cannabis, and methamphetamines markets. They also subcontract parts of the heroin trafficking process such as transportation and retail to other ethnic groups keeping wholesale to themselves. They also collaborate with native organized crime groups in Western Europe, such as British and British Asian groups, Dutch groups, as well as with Albanian crime groups, Pakistani groups, and Italian 'Mafia' groups. The fact that many of the Turkish organized criminals are now second generation migrants in Western Europe countries, and are more connected to the majority ethnic populations than their parents, facilitates this collaboration.

Apart from heroin and other drug trafficking and human smuggling, Turkish organized crime is heavily involved in debt collection, trafficking of women, cigarette smuggling, vehicle theft and trafficking, and currency counterfeiting. It engages in firearms and other offensive weapons smuggling, with many of these firearms and weapons ending up at the hands of the Kurdistan Workers' Party (PKK). Organized criminals are also involved in blackmailing and the extortion primarily of members of their communities in Western Europe. Furthermore, Turkish organized criminals have operated on behalf of legitimate businessmen to interfere with the public contract awards after the 1990s through violence or the threat of violence. Violence has been common with Turkish drug traffickers in particular. There have been cases involving kidnapping and torture, which are usually related to violation of internal, informal codes of conduct in the drug business, and despite the generally smooth collaboration, violence while competing for slices of the drugs retail markets is present with Turkish gangs affiliated to crime families. According to the British NCA, for example, from 2009 to 2015 there were nineteen violent incidents involving guns between the Bombaçilar ('Bombers'), a Turkish gang linked to the Baybaşin crime family, and their rivals, the Tottenham Boys, in north London.

Profits from criminal activities are invested in legal businesses such as restaurants, cafés, and fast food shops in Western Europe, real estate, particularly in London, Turkish football clubs, gambling venues, the tourist industry and real estate in the Mediterranean coast of Turkey and Turkish-occupied North Cyprus, as well as property, land, and factories in the criminals' area of origin. The offshore banking system of North Cyprus, with its bare-minimum

regulatory oversight, has been also been exploited by Turkish
organized crime to launder crime money.

Latin American organized crime

When one refers to 'Latin American organized crime' the first
thing that comes to mind is the Colombian and Mexican drug
cartels operating from the 1970s onwards. Of course, drug
trafficking in both Colombia and Mexico has a much longer
history. Drug cartels are essentially oligopolies: they are groups
of independent drug trafficking groups in specific geographic
regions, which pool their resources together. These drug cartels
are not the only form of organized crime in Colombia and Mexico,
and human smuggling and trafficking, among other ventures, are
also big business. Neither are Colombia and Mexico the only Latin
American countries in which organized crime is present. Drug
trafficking groups and prison gangs in Brazil or in Central
America offer similarly strong instances of organized crime. We
nevertheless focus on the Colombian and Mexican cartels because
of the great impact they have had on the international drug
market, and on the Colombian and Mexican societies, as well as
their capacity for extreme violence and government infiltration.

Colombian cartels rose to prominence in the 1970s when cocaine
replaced marijuana as the main illicit commodity of Colombia.
At the time, law enforcement efforts intercepted successfully the
smuggling of marijuana loads into the United States. The two
major Colombian cartels were Medellin and Cali, named after the
cities that were the centre of their activities, cities with a tradition
in illegal trades since the 19th century. The Medellin cartel was
led by the Ochoa brothers, Carlos Ledher, Jose Rodriguez Gacha,
and the notorious Pablo Escobar (Box 2), whereas the Cali cartel
was led by the Rodriguez-Orejuela brothers among others. The
cartels had a hierarchical, complex structure including branches
or subcontracted parties that handled aspects of the business,
such as security and counterintelligence, maintaining financial

Box 2 Pablo Escobar

Pablo Emilio Escobar Gaviria, also known as 'Don Pablo', 'El Patrón' (The Boss), and the 'King of Cocaine', was born on 1 December 1949. He started his criminal career as a car thief and marijuana trader. Due to the Medellin cartel's business Escobar managed to become one of the wealthiest people in the world, an achievement that was acknowledged by *Forbes* magazine. In 1982, Escobar was elected as an alternate deputy to the Colombian Congress; however, his political career was extremely short and ended when his involvement in the cocaine trade was revealed. Escobar was feared as a ruthless and often unpredictable criminal who introduced the dogma 'silver or lead' ('accept a bribe or get shot') in the Medellin cartel's business. He also contributed millions of dollars from the drug trade to charities and philanthropic ventures. Although it has been suggested that his activities aimed at creating a protective shield of popularity and a large support network for his drug business, he was considered a protector of the poor in his community. Because of his philanthropic work, which included the construction of schools, churches, and hospitals, he was even celebrated as a saint in some parts of the country. He enjoyed publicity and he even hired image makers to assist him in projecting a better image. Escobar ordered the assassination of the Colombian Minister of Justice, Rodrigo Lara Bonilla, in 1984. Bonilla had irritated Escobar by diverting governmental resources into the prosecution of traffickers mostly working for the Medellin cartel. In 1991, Escobar reached an agreement with the Colombian authorities, surrendering and accepting a five-year prison sentence in return for a promise that he would not be extradited to the United States. He escaped in transit during his removal to a correctional institution in July 1992. The Colombian authorities with the assistance of the US armed forces initiated a manhunt, which resulted in Escobar living as a fugitive and eventually being killed by Colombian police officers on 2 December 1993.

records or contract killings. They also established 'cells' in destination countries, such as the United States and Spain to handle distribution. In the late 1970s, drug trafficking by the cartels was responsible for up to 20 per cent of the money supply of Colombia. It has also been suggested that in the mid-1980s, their golden era, Colombian cartels were trading 80 per cent of the US cocaine market with annual profits of US$3 billion. Profits were laundered through legitimate businesses and the banking system. For example, the Bank of Credit and Commerce International (BCCI), a bank that became defunct in 1991 after investigations by financial regulators, pleaded guilty to charges of laundering money for the Colombian cartels.

The two cartels forged alliances with different segments of the Colombian society. The Medellin cartel established links with the army and supported the development of paramilitary groups to protect its investments in rural areas, whereas the Cali cartel established links with the police. The Medellin cartel was notorious for its use of kidnappings and its army of 3,000 assassins (*sicarios*) against competitors, informers, law enforcement officers, members of the judiciary, and politicians, as well as generally anyone who was considered an obstacle to their business. On the other hand, the Cali cartel, while it did use lethal violence especially against competitors, it also adopted a primarily entrepreneurial approach to cocaine smuggling, by investing on legitimate businesses including banks, televisions stations, and football clubs, and by creating a web of 'supporters' among journalists, law enforcement agents, and politicians through bribes.

The death of Pablo Escobar on the Medellin side in the early 1990s and the indictments of Cali cartel leaders meant the end of big Colombian cartel domination of the drugs market. Both cartels dissolved into smaller and much more flexible smuggling networks with self-contained parts (e.g. production, transportation, distribution), although important actors from the early cocaine scene, such as the Ochoa brothers, remained highly active at the wholesale level. This new structure of the drug trafficking business allowed traffickers to minimize risks by controlling the flow of information about drug smuggling. Put simply, if someone was arrested, he or she could not reveal information about other aspects of the process. At around the same time in the 1990s, the Revolutionary Armed Forces of Colombia (FARC), a leftist guerrilla force active since 1964, as well as right-wing paramilitary groups started using drug production and trafficking as major sources of income.

The demise of the Colombian cartels and the emergence of the Mexican cartels are closely linked. Successful US law enforcement efforts, resulting in the closure of the cocaine trafficking route through Florida, upgraded the role of Mexican traffickers. In the mid-1990s, the smuggling of Colombian cocaine into the US was through Mexico, after Mexican drug trafficking groups were subcontracted by Colombians. The latter retained the wholesale level, but also started setting up schemes for smuggling heroin into the United States. Mexican drug trafficking groups were paid US$1,000–2,000 per kilo of cocaine they transported. Because they were involved in the riskiest part of the smuggling process, they naturally demanded a bigger share of the profits. In the mid-1990s, the Mexicans changed from being subcontracted parties working for the Colombians to being equal partners. They took over wholesale in southern and western US states, while Colombians retained controlled over eastern states. In this way, the Mexican drug cartels were established.

The US Drug Enforcement Administration (DEA) has identified seven cartels (also referred to as 'drug trafficking organizations') in Mexico: Tijuana, Sinaloa, Juárez, Gulf, Los Zetas, Beltrán Leyva, and La Familia Michoacána. It has been suggested that these have now fragmented into as many as twenty, including more than 200 non-hierarchical cells disbanded from those organizations. More than 90 per cent of the cocaine (with an estimated value of US$30 billion per year) destined for the US is transported through Mexico. Mexican cartels are not only responsible for a significant part of the cocaine market in the US, but also for a significant segment of the heroin ('black tar' heroin), marijuana, and methamphetamine markets. Mexico is a major marijuana and opium source, and has also emerged as a big producer in methamphetamines. Profits are laundered through legitimate businesses primarily in Mexico. A key figure of the Sinaloa cartel, Ismael Zambada Garcia, for example, was reported to have a diverse financial portfolio including real estate, an aquatic park, a dairy company, and a bus firm.

A significant part of the violence that has plagued Mexico, especially since the mid-2000s, has been related to drug trafficking. The toll of drug-related violence from 2007 to 2014 was more than 50,000 murders, and approximately 26,000 men, women, and children missing. Some suggest that the 2004 expiration of the US Federal Assault Weapons Ban, which lifted the prohibition on sales of semi-automatic firearms to civilians, contributed to the deadly violence by allowing Mexican drug traffickers to have access to these firearms. While this development may have been instrumental, the presence of drug-related violence in Mexico nevertheless has to be seen within its political context. The authoritarian party Partido Revolucionario Institucional (PRI), which stayed in power uninterruptedly from 1929 to 2000, was particularly effective in creating informal coalitions with drug traffickers and others, which regulated and, in fact, protected the drug trade, especially until the late 1980s. Within this arrangement, specific drug traffickers were given permission to operate in a specific area in exchange for a share of the profits made. The state offered protection to drug traffickers, a relative order was imposed on the drug market, and at the same time the state profited from the business. When the candidate of the opposition party (Partido Acción Nacional), Vincente Fox, came to power in 2000, and replaced state officials who had forged relationships with drug traffickers, this equilibrium in the drugs trade was breached. Subsequently, under the aggressive

3. Cartel members arrested by the Mexican Army.

policy against drug traffickers under the government of Felipe Calderón between 2006 and 2012, violence reached terrifying levels, and was also of a different nature (Figure 3). Among the thousands of casualties were not only drug traffickers from competing cartels, but also police, public officials, members of the judiciary, and even music bands performing ballads celebrating drug trafficking and major traffickers (*narco-corridos*). The killings were expressive, with victims often being decapitated, castrated, or dismembered, and left in public view. Other cases involved the 'stewing' of victims. The killings or arrests of key cartel figures instead of pacifying the drug scene actually made the situation worse, since drug traffickers down the hierarchy fought fervently for vacant positions of power.

Chinese organized crime

Chinese organized crime has its roots to the Chinese secret societies that are now extinct. These secret societies were distinguished in religious and secular associations. The religious secret societies, such as the Patriarch Luo Cult, systematically engaged in acts of violence towards achieving political and religious objectives. The goal of the 'Heaven and Earth Society' (also known as 'Hung Mun'), for example, was to overthrow the Qing Dynasty and restore the Ming Dynasty. On the other hand, secular secret societies provided support to disadvantaged populations. Historical research has suggested that, as early as the final years of the Han Dynasty (206 BC–AD 220), poor peasants and street hawkers among others established clandestine 'organizations' to acquire resources. Secret societies had a hierarchical, secretive, and closely patriarchal structure; rituals; and followed a subculture that involved not only loyalty and solidarity, but also secret gestures and argot that were not accessible to outsiders. Importantly, these societies adhered to 'Oaths', 'Rules', and 'Commandments'.

In pre-communist China, the so called Shanghai Tycoons, who originated from the Green Gang, monopolized the illegal businesses of prostitution, drugs, and gambling in Shanghai before engaging in and controlling significant segments of the banking, shipping, and the food industries. In Mao-era China (1945–78) members of secret societies were imprisoned or executed, and the secret societies disappeared, even though they were present in other countries in Asia, America, and Europe. Since the economic reforms of 1978, which marked a transition to a more liberalized economic regime with immense opportunities for business and profit, similar criminal structures re-emerged.

Contemporary Chinese organized crime collectivities, particularly those involved in transnational criminal activities, include, first, *Hong Kong-based 'Triads'*. The term 'Triad' was coined by the British authorities based on the three essential elements, 'heaven, earth, man', represented on the early secret societies' banners. Triads are organizations that have a hierarchical structure and a name, a boss at the top, rituals of induction, argots, and gestures just like the older secret societies. Among the Triad groups, 14K and Sun Yee On are the most known and active. Second, they include *Taiwan-based crime groups* (such as the United Bamboo). The third category comprises *US-based 'Tongs'*, literally meaning 'halls' or 'gathering places'. These were initially gangs to defend Chinese migrants, and emerged in San Francisco in the 1850s. The core of Tong groups are hierarchical. Fourth, *US-based gangs* (members of which are often recruited by Triads for specific jobs); and, finally, *networks*. Networks do not involve a hierarchy, and the activity or the market in which individuals are engaged are simply an associational context. Many contemporary forms of organized crime such as counterfeiting, drug dealing, and human trafficking (the so called 'Snakeheads') are the business of networks and have nothing to do with structures such as seen in the Triads.

On the other hand, there is a parallel track of Chinese organized criminal activities, which are locally based. Despite the wide range of entities involved in Chinese organized crime, there is a tendency on the part of the politicians, law enforcement agencies, many academics, and the media to aggregate these entities into one category. In China, official documents and legislation use the term 'black societies' (*heishehui*) to refer to any criminal underworld structure.

Irrespectively of the structures behind specific illegal activities, illegal markets, and/or specific schemes, Chinese organized crime thrives upon several conditions and cultural characteristics, such as the *guanxi*. This refers to 'connections', or relationships between people, manifested in preferential treatment given to the partners in an exchange, which can take the form of access to resources, information, and protection. Establishing and nurturing *guanxi* is a business strategy developed by Chinese organized criminals to set up an illegal business, and to cope with the challenges associated with doing business in illegal markets such as debt collection, law enforcement action, and competitor activities.

The political element has been a very important part of Chinese organized crime. Although the government vehemently denies the existence of the criminal underworld in China, political and organized crime objectives have either been identical or co-existing. The 14K was originally established by nationalist party of China (Kuomintang) Lieutenant-General Kot Siu-wong; moreover, Sun Yat-Sen and Chiang Kai-Sek, the founder of the Kuomintang and its leader after World War II, were a few of the politicians who were allegedly lifelong 'members' of the Triads. Some Triads were in fact tolerated as 'good' and 'patriotic'. This 'political-criminal nexus' is either active, through clientelist relationships or bribery in the form of money, expensive gifts; and/or services; or passive, through personal, familial, and other links. It involves a synergy between the criminal 'underworld' and the political establishment, offering 'protective umbrellas' (*baohusan*). As a result, it undermines and sabotages the policing of organized criminals and their prosecution on a day-to-day basis. Criminal actors have captured local authorities including the police, the judiciary, and party and government figures. It also allows mainland Chinese criminal groups to infiltrate businesses and exploit them for their purposes. Some of these criminal groups exist as private companies. The blurring between organized criminal activities and the legal sector is reflected in the low rate of conviction for the more serious offences committed by the organized criminals who are covered behind legal businesses.

Apart from mainland China, Hong Kong, Macao, and Taiwan, contemporary Chinese organized criminals have been embedded in the sizable Chinese diaspora. They have been active in North and Latin America, Europe, South Africa, and the Asia-Pacific region, and have forged some alliances with indigenous groups. Chinese organized criminals are involved in predatory and violent crime, including homicides, armed robberies, looting, extortion, kidnappings, and contract killings of Chinese businessmen, as well as manipulation of legal markets, illegal gambling, illegal wildlife trade, fraud, firearms trafficking, drug trafficking, human smuggling and trafficking, and large-scale counterfeiting of a wide range of commodities (Figure 4).

4. Chinese official walking on counterfeit medicines.

Japanese organized crime

Japanese organized crime is synonymous with the term *Yakuza*. The term originates from the losing or lower score in the card game *oicho-kabu*, which is a version of the Western baccarat. The score, 8-9-3, is pronounced *ya-ku-za*, and it was probably adopted by Japanese criminals themselves in the early 20th century to connote their self-images as losers or outcasts from mainstream, respectable society. The Yakuza are a set of criminal organizations with ancient roots. There are two views about the history of the Yakuza. The first suggests that the Yakuza can be traced back in the 17th century's *kabuki-mono* (the 'mad ones'), a group of eccentric, in appearance and behaviour, samurai who terrorized and victimized local populations. The second view suggests that the Yakuza are the result partly of traditional Japanese cultural elements in association with the presence of peddlers and gamblers forming criminal gangs during the Edo era (1603–1868).

There is no single Yakuza, but a large number of strict, rule-following organized crime groups (also referred to as *Boryokudan*, 'the violent ones'), the most powerful groups being the Yamaguchi-Gumi, the Sumiyoshi-Kai, and the Inagawa-Kai. During the Yakuza group acme, after World War II, which corresponded with the growth of the Japanese economy, the number of Yakuza group members was more than 180,000. In the last five years or so, local laws have been introduced in all forty-seven prefectures of Japan targeting firms that knowingly conduct business with Yakuza groups in an attempt to deprive the groups of income. This has had a significant impact on official membership numbers, with the National Police Agency estimating a total of 58,600 Yakuza group members in 2013.

Significantly, unlike associations of a similar nature in other countries, the Yakuza groups are not necessarily outlawed. The first anti-gang law of Japan, which was introduced in 1992, allowed the police to designate a group as being an 'organized crime group' primarily on the basis of the proportion of convicted criminals among its members. Most groups put themselves forward as mutual aid societies with established commercial activities, and they are registered with the police. Reports have suggested that many of them have attempted to re-invent themselves as charitable organizations. For example, in the early 1990s, the Yamaguchi-Gumi re-established part of its organization as the National League to Purify the Land, a non-profit charity against drug abuse. Moreover, after the Tohoku earthquake and tsunami in March 2011, Yakuza rushed to the area with truckloads of emergency supplies for the local population and offered other resources (such as a helicopter) to the local authorities. Unlike other organized crime groups, which aim for a discreet presence, the Yakuza groups are not secret societies, and this is reflected on them having offices with signs in business and shopping districts, and their members having business cards. Yakuza members were elected to serve in various public offices in the past; many leaders of the Yakuza groups still occupy the status of a celebrity in the Japanese society; and numerous Yakuza fan magazines are in circulation.

Yakuza groups are among the most centralized in the world of organized crime. Their members are linked through elaborate hierarchies and, once initiated, they must subvert all other allegiances in favour of the Yakuza. The Yakuza follow the traditional Japanese hierarchical structure, which is patriarchal in its nature, and revolves around the idea of *Ikka* ('family'), and the fictive relationships *oyabun-kobun* ('father'- / 'head of the family'-'foster child') and *kyodaibun* ('brother-brother'). The *oyabun* is at the top of the hierachy. The second level includes the *waka gashira* ('first lieutenant') and the *shatei gashira* ('second lieutenant'); followed by the *kyodai* ('brothers') on the third level. However, in the Japanese organized crime scene there are some criminal gangs that collaborate or work as 'freelancers' for Yakuza groups. It should be noted that Yakuza groups are not always stable. They may emerge as a split from another group, or they may join a larger group. Although the Yakuza are rooted in Japanese society, many of their members are not Japanese. There is, for instance, a striking over-representation of ethnic Koreans among their ranks, including many 'heads of family'.

The Yakuza follow specific rituals. One of them involves, for instance, the *oyabun* and the new member drinking sake from the same cup as the other members in the initiation ceremony or exchanging sake cups. The most well-known ritual, however, is *yubitsume*, which involves a member cutting off the tip of their own small finger by way of apology in the case of a wrongdoing to a fellow member. A defining characteristic of Yakuza members are their impressive full-body tattoos known as *irezumi* (Figure 5).

The Yakuza groups as a whole have been heavily involved in a number of criminal activities such as (particularly synthetic) drug trafficking, gambling, extortion rackets including civil disputes mediation, blackmail, loansharking, prostitution, pornography, firearms trafficking, insurance fraud, credit card fraud, migrant smuggling, illegal dumping of industrial waste, and money laundering through legitimate businesses and casinos in Japan

5. Tattooed Yakuza at a shrine festival in Tokyo.

and abroad. Some of these groups are involved in an activity or a
market that may be prohibited to the members of another group.
The collapse of Japan's 'bubble economy' in the late 1980s to early
1990s, and its financial repercussions, pushed Yakuza groups to
conduct business in Southeast Asia as well as the United States,
and specifically Las Vegas, Atlantic City, and Hawaii, with the
latter being an important transit point between Japan and mainland
United States. The Yakuza have also made their presence known
in Australia and Russia. There is some evidence that Yakuza
groups cooperate with Russian criminals, Colombian criminals,
American crime groups including Italian-Americans, and Chinese
migrant smugglers (the Snakeheads, mentioned earlier).

The nature of the Yakuza and its embeddedness in Japanese
society has allowed groups to invest in legal businesses such as

night-time economy establishments and the construction industry in which they were traditionally present, and to become involved in financially sophisticated schemes, such as the securities exchange business. Moreover, they have been able to infiltrate important and functional businesses for the Japanese society. For example, in the late 1980s, the head of one of the largest groups, the Inagawa-Kai, bought US$250 million worth of Tokyo Electric Railway's stock. Yakuza groups have traditionally had close ties with politicians of the extreme right especially since the 1930s, and they were even used by the Liberal Democratic Part of Japan to break left-wing demonstrations and labour unions. In June 2007, the 40,000-member Yamaguchi-gumi and 10,000-member Inagawa-Kai decided to fully and publicly support the country's second political party, the Democratic Party of Japan.

Outlaw motorcycle gangs

Outlaw Motorcycle Gangs (OMGs) firstly appeared in the United States after World War II and comprised mostly of returning war veterans who found it difficult to adjust to 'mainstream' civilian life, and rejected its values and norms. The adjective 'outlaw' does not refer to groups violating the law, but those motorcycle groups that are not recognized by the official motorcyclist associations, such as the American Motorcyclist Association (AMA), and do not follow their rules. OMGs are also referred to as 'one percenters', meaning that they belong to the 1 per cent of motorcycle groups that are 'rebels' compared to the 99 per cent that are 'conformists'. OMGs became known to the public after an incident on 4th July 1947 in Hollister, California. The incident involved members of the the Pissed Off Bastards of Bloomington (POBOB), who, among other motorcycle gangs, raced their bikes through the streets of the small town, drinking excessive amounts of beer, and 4,000 bikers protesting against the arrest of a 'brother' for 'public indecency'.

In the 1950s and early 1960s, OMGs spread outside California. Some members of POBOB split from their group and established the Hells Angels (note: no apostrophe on 'Hells') with local branches, known as 'chapters', in the rest of the country. In addition, new OMGs were established throughout the United States. From the late 1960s onwards, more than 300 Hells Angels 'chapters' were created around the world including the Brazilian Amazon and Liechtenstein. According to Europol, the only European country that does not have OMGs is Cyprus. In some counties, such as Norway, Sweden, and Denmark, the very term 'organized crime' was initially used in relation to the clubs Hells Angels and Bandidos in the early 1990s.

The general view of law enforcement agencies internationally is that OMGs are highly structured. This is partly true. Some OMGs are hierarchical and involve a 'chapter' president; a vice-president; a treasurer responsible for the group's finances; a sergeant-at-arms who enforces discipline; a road captain, who acts as the club's runs manager mapping out routes, taking care of refuelling stops, etc.; and associate members. These OMGs have an international presence through their 'chapters'. The biggest and most powerful OMGs, also known as the 'Big Four', are the Hells Angels, the Bandidos, the Outlaws, and the Pagans. These OMGs are at the top of the biker world hierarchy. The vast majority of OMGs, however, are regional, rather disorganized, and with a small membership. Others are satellite and support groups (the 'hangaround' clubs), they are controlled by the bigger OMGs and constitute a pool for potential members.

Membership is controlled: prospective members must be nominated by an existing member and complete a probationary period, which commonly lasts for up to a year. Within the probation period, members have to prove their loyalty to the group. They pay monthly dues and follow rules and a specific code of conduct. For instance, they are not allowed to inject drugs and fight each other with weapons; and they are expected to support other members. Members also wear the distinctive sleeveless leather or denim patched jacket with the name of the club, logo,

6. Hells Angels' sleeveless patched jackets, also referred to as 'colours'.

and location, also referred to as 'colours' (Figure 6). Patches as well as tattoos provide information about a member's personal, criminal, and even sexual history. For instance, a purple wings patch on a member's jacket signifies someone who had oral sex with a female corpse. Women, also known as 'mamas' or 'sheep' in the biker vernacular, are not at the core of OMGs and cannot become members. However, unlike their counterparts in earlier biker groups, who were simply involved in group parties and were at best sexual partners, women are now involved in economic and criminal activities for their partners or the whole biker group.

Generally, OMGs tend to receive disproportionate attention by the police and other authorities because of their way of life. Although becoming a member of an OMG is very rarely a result of a desire to commit crimes, and members of OMGs should not be viewed as a homogenous group when it comes to criminality, criminal activities are committed by many members albeit not necessarily within the organizational structure of the OMG. For some clubs, and this is especially the case with the 'Big Four', it has been suggested that isolation from mainstream society, strong bonds between members, and loyalty to the group is a significant catalyst for the involvement of OMG members in organized criminal activities, which are an important source of income. Within some clubs, money and power provided by organized crime has become the major goal. In this context, satellite and support group clubs, which are controlled by the bigger OMGs, are often tasked with performing certain criminal activities for the bigger groups. Moreover, groups or individuals who are unaffiliated with OMGs may be subcontracted to perform a service in the process of committing a crime or managing the money from the activity.

In the 1980s, links between OMGs and 'traditional' US organized crime groups, such as the Gambino crime family, were identified, although the nature of this link is difficult to assess. The OMGs' primary business is the production and trading of synthetic drugs, particularly methamphetamines. A US government survey found that OMGs controlled 75 per cent of the methamphetamine market of the country in the 1990s. In this trade, there is cooperation between OMGs, and between OMGs and street gangs that cover the retail market in specific areas. OMGs are also involved in prostitution, small arms trafficking, motorcycle theft and trafficking, receiving stolen goods, and contract killings. In recent years, OMGs in Australia have expanded their activities to the trafficking of exotic animals. Profits from OMG criminal activities are invested in and laundered through escort- and prostitution-related businesses, massage parlours, pawn shops, and motorcycle repair shops among other legitimate businesses.

Reputation for violence is integral and instrumental to some of the OMG activities such as extortion, robberies, and debt collection. There have also been significant outbursts of violence between OMGs in Scandinavian countries, the United States, Canada, Australia, Germany, and Ireland, and in the context of drug trafficking. What was perhaps significant in the OMG-related violence in some contexts was that this was open and often involved firearms. In the 1990s, for example, the predominately Danish feud between the Hells Angels and the Bandidos spilled over to Norway, Sweden, and Finland, and it became known to the media as the 'Nordic biker war'. The 'war' saw the use of rocket launchers and hand grenades, and cost eleven lives and many more casualties. The Quebec Biker War over access to the Port of Montreal that was crucial for the drug trafficking business, involved numerous OMGs, although primarily Hells Angels and Rock Machine; lasted between 1994 and 2002; and resulted in 160 deaths including the death of bystanders.

Overall, our brief overview of organized crime structures in relation to their national context and locale must have shown the difficulty of reaching general statements about the nature of the phenomenon. Not all the three dimensions of organized crime that we have considered in the introduction are relevant in every case. In some cases, the existence and outlook of criminal groups draws on strong historical roots, whose influence is more pronounced in traditionalist contexts. On the other hand, a key factor in the evolution and survival of organized crime has to do with the presence of illicit market opportunities. In other cases, the blurring of the boundaries between organized crime and legitimate authority in a country or locale makes it less straightforward to understand the phenomenon as an instance of extra-legal governance. In search of more conclusive insights, in Chapter 3 we turn to a different entry point to the phenomenon, namely the consideration of specific activities or areas of activity of organized criminality.

Chapter 3
The business of organized crime

In Chapter 2, we briefly surveyed the variations which locale and cultural context impose on the structures of organized crime. In this chapter, our aim is to take a bolder step into the description and understanding of the phenomenon. We speak of the business of organized crime as this offers an important clue about the over-arching theme that readers will not find difficult to recognize: identifying the opportunities for financial gain, and organizing for participation, competition, and survival in illicit markets accounts for much of what is involved in organized crime. This characteristic means that our discussion is necessarily selective. We offer an overview of some prominent areas of activity for organized crime but our readers should be aware that the combination of a prospect for financial gain and the existence of a legal prohibition is a uniquely powerful motor for innovation.

Drug trafficking

Drug trafficking is considered the archetypal organized criminal activity, and drug markets the archetypal illegal markets, but this has not always been the case. In the past, the drug trade was a legitimate and a highly important economic activity. In the 19th century the opium trade in China was a significant source of profit for British companies. Heroin was sold by the pharmaceutical company Bayer as a medicine for a number of illnesses in the late

19th and early 20th centuries. For a variety of reasons, including moral and religious ones, states intervened in drug markets and drove significant segments of them into the domain of the illicit and clandestine. Early limited efforts to control drug use and trade on a local and national level can be found in the late 19th century. The Shanghai Opium Conference of 1909 and the subsequent International Opium Convention signed in The Hague in 1912 launched an international campaign against production, supply, and use of drugs.

Markets of (illegal) drugs cater for a large clientele, especially if those who have bought drugs infrequently or even just once are included. A proportion of this clientele are willing customers that use specific types of drugs recreationally and in the context of specific entertainment settings (e.g. ecstasy pills in the dance and rave scene). Others, such as heroin users, remain in the market due to addiction. Approximately 250 million people aged 15 to 64 have used drugs at least once in the last twelve months, the vast majority of them being recreational drug users.

Drug trafficking has been considered the biggest and most lucrative illegal economic sector—even more profitable than many legal trades. Reports suggest, for instance, that the drug trade is worth US$400 billion a year, or 8 per cent of all international trade, when motor-vehicle trade makes up only 5.3 per cent of all international trade. Some caution, however, is necessary, since figures on drug trafficking and drug markets are often spontaneously produced, or even invented to serve political agendas. Economically speaking, but also with regard to their nature, there are four main submarkets of drugs: namely the *cannabis* market, the biggest drug market worldwide, the *cocaine* market, the *heroin* market, and the *synthetic drugs* market.

Cannabis (herb and resin) is largely produced within the countries of consumption. Morocco, Afghanistan, and Mexico stand out as large producers and exporters. Colombia, Bolivia, and Peru are responsible for almost all production of coca (the basis of cocaine), whereas Afghanistan and Myanmar (Burma) are the biggest producers of opium (the basis of heroin) in the world. Significant quantities of opium are produced in India for the domestic market, while Mexico is a relatively big producer supplying primarily North American markets. Synthetic drugs, such as ecstasy/MDMA, amphetamines, and methamphetamines, are produced in various countries for domestic consumption and exportation (e.g. the Netherlands, Belgium, and the United Kingdom), and regions that produce drugs primarily for exportation, such as the Middle East and Southeast Asia.

When drugs are produced in countries other than the consumption countries, trafficking involves the importation/transportation of drugs across borders by land, air, or sea. Larger quantities are trafficked through normal commercial channels such as container shipping or haulage companies under the guise of international trade. The volume of trade via big ports throughout the globe makes detection difficult. In the transportation process from the production to the distribution countries, there are important transit countries. For example, significant cocaine quantities enter Western Europe via Spain, and heroin via Turkey. Smaller quantities have also been ordered online from underground ('dark net') websites, such as Silk Road and Silk Road 2.0, which have now been shut by the authorities, and so they are delivered by post.

Overall, excluding the phases of production and importation, there are three levels in drug trafficking: (a) wholesale, (b) middle-level, and (c) retail. There are, however, individuals who do not fit in one of these levels, simply because they are peripherally involved in the business by being subcontracted, for example, to transport a quantity of the merchandise, or by acting as intermediaries bringing together two disconnected parties in the business. The quantities of drugs imported in a country are broken into smaller quantities and sold to middle-level dealers, who in turn sell to retail dealers. Drugs are distributed to consumers in open markets, such as streets and public spaces, closed markets (e.g. houses, apartments), and through closed networks (e.g. groups of friends, music scenes, gyms).

There is no central control of drug trafficking internationally. Drug trafficking schemes present a great diversity in the way they are structured and how they operate, their size as well as the social background of their participants. In some contexts, specific parts of drug markets may be controlled by hierarchical structures that involve an importer/boss holding control of an area; underbosses; small-scale wholesalers; and retailers. The presence of a hierarchical structure (or the lack thereof) involved in drug trafficking schemes depends on a number of factors. First, the more an operation is 'transnational' in scope, the less likely it is that traffickers and dealers are part of a hierarchical structure. Trafficking cocaine from Colombia, for example, via a transit point in Africa to a locality in Germany will require groups and individuals that do not work for a boss. Moreover, very importantly, the presence of endemic corruption seems to be a critical factor for the creation of hierarchical structures in drug trafficking, as it happens, for instance, in Colombia and Mexico.

Generally, drug trafficking is mostly based on small, flexible, ephemeral, and opportunistic networks of traders. Drug markets are highly competitive environments involving mostly horizontal structures with a range of actors, who most often do not meet the criteria of the 'cartel barons' celebrated in the media. Indeed, a close look at the profiles of drug marketers can reveal the participation of bouncers, youngsters, teenagers 'having a good time' in the night-time economy, transporters, couriers, respectable professionals (legal entrepreneurs, lawyers, celebrities), 'user-dealers', and many others. Because of the high fragmentation of the drug markets and the various layers involved in the distribution of drugs, the dealers' income especially at the retail level is almost never as high as the media and law enforcement portray it to be. Calculations on crack-house dealer profits, for instance, support the conclusion that they get between US$7 and US$8 an hour. The vast majority of drug traffickers known to the authorities (90 per cent) are male.

An important aspect of the issues relating to drug trafficking has been the role of minority ethnic groups and immigrants, 'outsiders', and members of subcultures, and the level of control they exert. Despite the gaps in the available evidence, media, public, and authorities have been fascinated and obsessed with Colombian involvement in the cocaine trade on an international level, for example, or with the 'dominant position' on the control of the heroin market by Turkish 'organized crime groups'. There is a high involvement of specific ethnic groups in specific drug trafficking schemes, which is facilitated by the lack of alternatives and the presence of an ethnic group in a specific drug producing country. It is, however, extremely difficult for specific ethnic groups to monopolize and dominate the business due to the 'openness' and multi-ethnic nature of the drug markets, the need for protection from law enforcement agencies, and the need for individuals with capital, skills, connections, and so on.

Drug trafficking has been linked with other social problems such as deaths, public health (HIV, hepatitis, etc.), acquisitive crime, and social and criminal justice costs. Moreover, drug markets have been associated with forms violence that are often deadly, as well as armed conflict. The relationship is complex. It may be the case, for example, that the trafficking of drugs, especially in cities in South America and the Caribbean, is heavily related to urban violence, but the outlook of poverty is also a catalyst to this trend. Mexico's and Brazil's extremely high homicide rates are indicative of the violent practices embedded in some drug markets. There have been accounts that link drug trafficking with paramilitary and separatist groups. For example, the FARC and the Kurdish Workers' Party (PKK) have been involved in cocaine and heroin trafficking, respectively, to

7. **Boys harvesting poppy sap (raw opium) in the fields of Afghanistan.**

fund their activities. Drug trafficking and drug markets, however, can be embedded in the local communities and normalized. In fact, drug markets and economies are not only responsible for problematic issues and trends, but they can also offer something back to the (local) community. In rural areas of Afghanistan, for example, poppy cultivation is the only source of revenue (Figure 7).

Migrant smuggling

Irregular migration has been linked with the smuggling of migrants, a phenomenon that intensified from the early 1990s onwards. According to the United Nations' 2000 Protocol Against the Smuggling of Migrants by Land, Sea, and Air, smuggling of migrants is

> the procurement, in order to obtain, directly or indirectly, a
> financial or other material benefit, of the illegal entry of a person
> into a State Party of which the person is not a national or a
> permanent resident.

Smuggling is often confused with the trafficking of migrants. Smuggling, however, does not involve the exploitation of the smuggled individuals, and it is an offence against the legal framework of migration of the transit and destination countries, and an offence against the public order. There are three integral elements shaping the smuggling of migrants, namely, push factors, such as poverty, authoritarian regimes, wars and civil conflicts, corruption, environmental deterioration as well as demographic pressures; pull factors, such as the relative financial and political stability of the destination countries and demand for cheap labour, and finally facilitating factors, such as the media, the advancement of transportation means, the opening up of the economy and the mobility of capital, labour and commodities, historic/colonial links, and the existence of social networks among migrant communities. The role of the rigid legal framework of destination and transit countries should not be overlooked, as this is the prime reason prospective migrants seek the assistance of migrant smugglers to enter transit and destination countries.

Not all irregular migration is 'facilitated'. A significant percentage of irregular migrants, however, resort to the services of smugglers for at least a part of the journey. It is difficult to provide an accurate number of people whose irregular migration is facilitated. This is due to a variety of reasons, from the hidden nature of smuggling of migrants, and the consequent under-reporting of smuggling activities, the widely diverse set of methods of recording data on smuggling of migrants, often involving the use of two statistical concepts such as the 'stock' of irregular migrants at a given time and the 'flows' or irregular migrants. Moreover, the authorities, primarily in the transit countries, may turn a blind eye to migrant smuggling activities considering them as a way of diverting a large number of migrants out of their jurisdiction. Some estimates exist. For example, according to United Nations Office on Drugs and Crime (UNODC), approximately 55,000 migrants are smuggled from Africa into the EU per year.

Migrant smuggling is usually committed by small groups that have familial, friendship, and ethnic ties, and, in some cases, individuals, especially when there is no need for great sophistication in the smuggling operation. It could be safely argued that when it comes to the smuggling of Asian and African migrants, all smuggling groups and/or individuals 'cooperate' (without even being conscious of it) in an attempt to bring the bulk of migrants from Asia and Africa to Western Europe. This takes place via a smuggler-to-smuggler approach that does not allow irregular migrants to be lost. This chain, however, is sometimes broken during the journey, for example due to police operations, and then other individuals, groups, and networks that have no connection with the smugglers of the initial stage take over the process.

There is a division of duties and tasks in migrant smuggling schemes, although many times the tasks that each participant has to carry out differ from operation to operation, from time to time, from place to place, and from group to group. Sometimes a member of a smuggling group may have more than one duty. Still, there are some 'roles' within each group that may remain relatively stable over time, even though this does not necessarily mean that they exist in every smuggling scheme.

The *organizer* has a 'managerial' position in the group, and is concerned with the planning of the operation facilitating migration. He or she is not necessarily a hardened criminal, but is often is a legitimate entrepreneur (e.g. a travel agent) attempting to make additional profit. On many occasions he or she invests capital in the operation, for example, by making sure that the transportation means are available for the journey. For instance, in North Western Africa, *pateras*, small wooden boats with outboard motors, are bought by organizers for €3,000 each for the smuggling of migrants to the Canary Islands.

Recruiters, in the majority of the cases, are individuals who live permanently in the country of origin of the migrants or the transit country, and have a very good knowledge of the language, and the peculiarities of each country or specific locale, or even know the migrants personally. They also collect the initial fees for the transportation of the irregular migrants. In many cases the recruiters, and specifically those in the transit countries, are smuggled migrants themselves.

The *transporters/guides* are concerned with transferring, or at least assisting, migrants in the journey. There may be more than one transporter throughout the whole journey, or one for every country that needs to be crossed. There may also be a number of transporters/guides even within the same country.

In addition, there are *service providers* responsible for providing various services and, most importantly, accommodation to migrants while they wait to be smuggled to either another location within a country or to another country. Such service providers are useful for the smuggling groups and networks, particularly in those cases when small groups of migrants need to be gathered before they are transported to the next destination. The service providers are either local people or migrants, who have lived in the country for a considerable length of time. Other types of service providers such as document forgers and travel agents are also present in smuggling schemes. In many cases the service providers are opportunists, aiming to make a quick gain from their involvement in the process.

A further important role is that of the *corrupt public officials*, that is, those who either provide assistance during the smuggling process (e.g. employees in embassies and consulates in countries of origin and/or employees of authorities providing documentation) or others who are being bribed to turn a blind eye (e.g. corrupt police officers, port police officers, etc.).

According to UNODC, the process of facilitating irregular migration is 'pre-organized', basically meaning that irregular migrants do not negotiate with local facilitators during the journey as a chain of individuals who act independently. Rather, in close cooperation they carry out those negotiations with local facilitators, who are paid by the 'organizers'. It is not unusual, however, for migrants to receive an ad hoc facilitation of their migration in the form of a short transportation within a country after they started their journey on their own, and in some cases legally (e.g. Chinese migrants may travel to Western countries legally but continue their journey illegally).

In the case of human smuggling, it is usually the clients who approach the smuggler usually through their social circle in the source, and sometimes in the transit countries. Transportation can be on foot through unguarded passages in the borders, by trucks or cars with special crypts, and planes. Since the late 1990s to early 2000s the maritime smuggling of humans has become a prominent trend in human smuggling. The reasons are the larger profits for the smugglers, because maritime smuggling involves a larger number of clients per operation; the lack of need for great sophistication in the operation; and the smaller risks for smugglers, especially when they do not board the vessels with the migrants. Apart from these reasons, however, the trend is also due to the extremely long coastline of a number of destination and transit countries (e.g. in the Mediterranean Sea), which makes it impossible for it to be rigorously and effectively policed. Generally, the maritime smuggling of migrants, just as the smuggling of migrants by land and/or air, follows the pattern of migration, from East to West and South to North, and from relatively poor to relatively rich countries. The choice of the country of destination is significantly affected by the funds that are available for the journey.

As mentioned earlier, irregular migrants, or their families, who very often see the facilitation of their migration as an investment, pay the full or at least 50 per cent of the total smuggling fee in advance. This percentage of the fee is in most occasions used towards paying important actors of the journey before the actual journey starts. The rest of the fee is paid upon arrival in the destination country. In many occasions advance payments are made to a middle person, a trusted and prominent member of the local community, who then forwards the payment to the organizer upon the completion of the migrants' facilitated journey. Payments are made in cash in powerful currencies, and, in some instances, involve property (e.g. vehicles, houses, land, and jewellery). In many cases, prospective smuggled migrants borrow money from local money lenders. In addition, there are occasions in which migrants enter into debt bondage with the smuggler promising that they will pay back the debt once work is found at the country of destination. Smuggling fees vary considerably and depend on the distance and modes of transportation; the complexities of the journey, which are often associated with additional services by travel agencies; the authorities' efforts, documents forgers, and accommodation providers; the guarantees included; and the nationality of the migrants.

Human trafficking

According to article 3 of the *Protocol to Prevent, Suppress and Punish Trafficking in Persons, especially Women and Children* ('Trafficking Protocol') supplementing the 2000 United Nations Convention against Transnational Organized Crime, trafficking in persons is

the recruitment, transportation, transfer, harbouring or receipt of persons, by means of the threat or use of force or other forms of coercion, of abduction, of fraud, of deception, of the abuse of power or of a position of vulnerability or of the giving or receiving of payments or benefits to achieve the consent of a person having control over another person, for the purpose of exploitation'. Exploitation includes, 'at a minimum, the exploitation of the prostitution of others or other forms of sexual exploitation, forced labour or services, slavery or practices similar to slavery, servitude or the removal of organs.

Due to the nature and the increasing prevalence of the issue, heavy emphasis has been laid on victimization, as victims typically experience slavery-like conditions, serious abuse, and even life-threatening situations. Victimization has been a focal point of efforts by government agencies, NGOs, and IGOs, resulting in the two mains forms of victimization, sexual exploitation and forced labour, being relatively more visible and thus detectable than other forms of human trafficking, such as organ removal. According to UNODC, trafficking for sexual exploitation accounted for 58 per cent of all detected human trafficking worldwide in 2010, followed by forced labour (36 per cent). Furthermore, victims of human trafficking are predominantly women (59 per cent), followed by children (27 per cent), and then men (14 per cent). The proportion of female to male victims, adults to children, appears to have been decreasing in the past decade. Nevertheless, the above profile of the victim population underscores trafficking for sexual exploitation as the most prevalent form of contemporary human trafficking.

Reliable information on the structures and operations of trafficking groups has been less readily available, as it typically depends on case studies as well as on offender profiles drawn from prosecution and conviction data. At any rate, complaints about the quality and depth of information are not uncommon, and, while this situation is typically attributed to the clandestine nature of the activity, the involvement of a multiplicity of actors holding diverse positions towards the issue means that the process of generating relevant knowledge is not immune from important conceptual and thus, inevitably, factual biases.

Human trafficking is not necessarily a transnational crime. Domestic trafficking is also recognized as an issue affecting nationals of the country in which the activity takes place. When trafficking is a transnational crime, involving offenders and victims of different nationalities, it is best understood as a process embedded in contemporary migration flows. This first means that a 'push-pull' type of explanation that is more widely applicable to migratory movements can also account for the availability of a risk population in the countries of origin, and it also fits well the general direction of trafficking routes. This type of explanation can be found in official accounts of the issue.

Within the wider process of migration, human trafficking is itself a process distinguished by harmful situations and outcomes: essentially, trafficking can be thought as a migratory event that results in a form of harm. At least three phases can be distinguished: a) *recruitment*; b) *transportation* from the place of origin to the place of destination and potentially the illegal entry of the trafficked person; and c) the *exploitation* phase, during which the victim is forced into sexual or labour servitude. The nature of the process leaves a significant margin for uncertainty as to whether trafficking has genuinely taken place. From a victim-centred viewpoint the process may result in a non-harmful outcome, even though an illegal situation exists (e.g. illegal prostitution of adult migrants), or, conversely, the elements of force, coercion, or deception must be present in a trafficking situation. From the viewpoint of the offending behaviour, the grey area involved concerns the element of organization, since engaging in the trafficking process does not require crossing the particular organizational threshold introduced, for example, by the UN Convention ('structured group of three or more persons', 'non randomly formed'). This organizational element may not be present when, for example, individuals contribute to different phases of the process in an isolated and opportunistic fashion or within loose networks, in which case it must be constructed analytically, following research or detection of the activity. Evidently, this allows for a more complicated typology of actors and, therefore, a degree of uncertainty, particularly at the lower organizational end of criminal activity involving loose networks and 'un-organized' criminal involvement. Also, the commission of associated crimes, which, depending on a national legal system, would include such crimes as involuntary servitude, forced or compulsory labour, unlawful coercion, unlawful threats, extortion, false imprisonment,

8. 'You are not a commodity'. Billboard in Moldova.

kidnapping, illegal procurement, corruption, debt bondage, document theft, destruction or forgery of documents, sexual assault, assault, bodily injury, rape, etc., does not necessarily indicate an organized crime activity, even if the 'serious crime' requirement is fulfilled. The upshot of the above conceptual qualifications is that measuring the magnitude of the issue in financial terms (turnover, profits) is far from straightforward, since not all financially significant activity can be indiscriminately characterized as organized-crime related (Figure 8).

Viewing human trafficking as a business process permits the identification of the three general phases of recruitment, transportation, and exploitation, in which financial inputs and outputs are involved and, therefore, different actors may play a financially significant role. These actors may belong to more robust organizational forms featuring hierarchical structures, or operate within stronger or looser networks whether as individuals or as part of smaller groups carrying out different functional parts (recruitment, transport, protection, marketing) of the activity in one or in different phase of the process. According to UNODC, apart from traffickers themselves, a variety of actors can be involved in the process. They can be individuals who may or may not belong to an organization and who commit or are complicit in the commission of trafficking offences, and also criminals operating peripherally to trafficking and facilitating the commission of trafficking.

Recruitment, excluding the event of abduction of the victim, is known to be facilitated by such diverse actors as friends and family of the victims, travel bureaus, employment agencies, or even artistic management companies and international marriage agencies. Traffickers may use legitimate agencies, but even when an illegitimate front is used, they may present to the victim contracts and legal documentation as a means of alleviating any concerns about trafficking and masking the intended exploitation. Forging documents or obtaining the necessary documents possibly by means of corruption and bribery of law enforcement or other officials is a possibility at this stage.

Transportation, including the stage of harbouring the victims in transit, is also a phase in which different actors performing different functions accordingly (drivers, guides, boat owners, hotel owners, landlords, bodyguards) may be involved. The financial significance is that the involvement of a variety of actors entails transactions that cannot be indiscriminately considered as part of an 'organized crime' activity.

Exploitation constitutes the core criminal activity, and, again, it may involve a typology of actors carrying out functional parts of the process. Sex trafficking victims can be highly visible and forced to engage in street-level prostitution. In many cases, sex trafficking takes place in underground venues, such as private homes or brothels. Public and legal locations such as massage parlours, spas, and strip clubs also act as fronts for illegal prostitution and trafficking. Similarly, forced labour has been detected in labour intensive manufacture (e.g. textiles), construction and agriculture.

Illegal trade in tobacco

The illegal trade in tobacco is a manifestation of organized crime with a long history which relatively recently began receiving much academic attention. There are four main types of schemes characterizing this trade in the last two decades. The first is *bootlegging*—buying a quantity of cigarettes that exceeds custom regulations. Bootlegging schemes, which abuse cross-border shopping, involve individual entrepreneurs and small groups of entrepreneurs smuggling small quantities of cigarettes when on holiday in or visiting countries with relatively cheaper cigarettes. In the US, there is the distinct feature of interstate bootlegging, and bootlegging from Native American reservations.

The second type of scheme is *large-scale smuggling* of untaxed cigarettes diverted from licit international trade. This type of smuggling depends on an interaction with licit businesses (who wittingly or unwittingly participate) and are embedded in the legal business processes.

The third type is *counterfeiting* or the manufacturing of fake brand cigarettes. A source country for counterfeit cigarettes destined for the EU market is China. After aggressive and effective crackdowns against cigarette smuggling and domestic distribution channels, the Chinese illegal cigarette industry shifted to exporting large numbers of counterfeit Western brand cigarettes to black markets abroad including many EU markets and most notably the UK. China emerged as a leading supplier of counterfeit cigarettes in the EU and beyond as a result of the contradictions of the economic reform process and of external licit and illicit forces that worked toward opening up the Chinese tobacco sector to the outside world. In recent years there have been reports about counterfeit cigarettes being produced in countries such as Ukraine, Poland, and Greece, and closer to the destination markets within the European Union.

Finally, apart from legally manufactured cigarettes, which are stolen from legal premises (retail markets, supermarkets, kiosks, etc.) before they are introduced in the illegal market as well as online sales of legally produced tobacco products, there is a relatively recent phenomenon which involves legally produced tobacco products manufactured in free zones of eastern Europe, United Arab Emirates (UAE), Malaysia, and South Africa, and which are readily available to illegal marketers. The most known case in the European market is Jin Ling, a brand lawfully manufactured in the free zone of Kaliningrad (Russia), but destined for the EU's illegal market.

A variety of methods have been employed towards getting to know the extent of the illegal trade in tobacco products. These include customs seizure data, smoker surveys, empty pack and cigarette butt collection analysis, household surveys of tobacco products consumption as well as governmental and trade monitoring data. Some estimates suggest that up to 600 billion cigarettes a year are illegal—smuggled, counterfeit, or tax-evaded in other ways—constituting 12 per cent of world consumption. There is a wide diversity in the percentage of illegally traded tobacco products among contexts. For instance, although the EU-27 average of illegally traded tobacco products is 9.9 per cent, there are extremes such as Lithuania (40.7 per cent of the overall tobacco products market) and Cyprus (0.6 per cent of the overall market). The figures need to be treated cautiously. Illegal markets involve economic activities that are intended to go unnoticed and thus remain unrecorded in the official statistics. Some data are produced and indeed presented here; however, this reflects the intensity and success/failure of law enforcement operations as well as the weaknesses of the methods mentioned earlier rather than the actual extent of the illicit market in the European Union.

Much of the tobacco-related criminal entrepreneurial conduct presented in media, and law enforcement and industry narratives has been cast in the rhetoric of 'transnational organized crime', a phrase with much mystique and threat imagery. The available evidence from a variety of contexts shows that a substantial part of the distribution market is covered by somewhat older, lower middle-class individuals, who are not hardened career criminals and are not involved in a diverse set of criminal activities. Most of those are action-oriented individuals, who in most instances act for their personal interests and often on improvization. The closer one gets to those cigarette smugglers, the more the stereotypical 'organized criminal' image dissolves. Illegal cigarette entrepreneurs can be the most 'unusual suspects', who would definitely not fit the profile of the archetypal smuggler. The composition of the group of transporters, the groups mostly involved with the authorities, looks more varied with many network relationships, individuals keen on getting a piece of the market and very few 'organizations' characterized by a more sophisticated division of labour. At the core of collaboration between and among entrepreneurs often lie family or kinship relationships as well as relationships forged within legal businesses (e.g. employer–employee, business partners, etc.). Violence and threat of violence are rare as they attract unnecessary attention and are, therefore, bad for business.

Generally, and excluding actors that are not involved in the business per se (e.g. corrupt public officials), the major players in the business can be distinguished in, first, the *manufacturers* who, in most cases, are based are based outside the country where the illegal trade takes place. Nevertheless, in some countries it is not unusual for the merchandise to be legally produced in the country and, using fictitious exportation schemes, re-introduced in the country of origin and its illegal market. These manufacturers can operate a legal business or an illegal one, as in the case of Chinese counterfeiters.

Second, *importers* and *wholesalers* are those entrepreneurs who have the capital to invest in the illegal cigarette market. Similarly to other illegal trades, importers and wholesalers tend to absorb most costs relating to the business and the risks associated with it, for example, the seizure or loss of the merchandise, transportation between/among countries, bribes of officials. As they are primarily situated in the domain of legal business, they have a range of options towards financing a scheme. These include, first, savings and capital from the legal business. While, the available evidence largely suggests that there is very little 'commodity hopping', it not unusual for this type of entrepreneurs at this level to re-invest capital obtained from other illegal markets. For example, there have been cases of entrepreneurs being involved simultaneously in cigarette smuggling and the smuggling of other commodities such as fuel and medicines or alcohol.

Third, the *retailers* constitute a category that includes travelling individuals (tourists, students, etc.) driven by the price disparities between/among countries. Individual smugglers could also be labelled as *occasional smugglers*, presented with a one-off smuggling opportunity in a trip abroad, and others who could be described as *regulars*, having a different temporal horizon to their business. Small (legal) shop-owners and street-sellers may also fall within this category. The retailers have the smallest profit margins, first because the bootleggers buy the merchandise with a slightly increased price given that the taxation—as a 'price wedge'—is included. Second, the retailers associated with wholesalers/importers and pushers either work for them, or, in case they buy the product, a part of the overall profit is primarily absorbed by people in the other echelons of the business. Financing the business at this level does not require significant amounts. This usually involves amounts obtained from the legal business or small savings as a start-up capital which is re-invested in the illegal tobacco trade in cycles depending on the varying volume of sales. Given that their legal business is also the outlet for their illegal business, retailers of that nature do not have substantial operational costs. For some retailers, such as those who own a legal business selling cigarettes or other commodities, the illicit trade of tobacco products is a means of increasing income. For some other retailers and specifically those involved in street-selling, who very often are migrants, socio-economic marginalization is the common characteristic and the illicit tobacco trade is one of the very few employment options available.

Counterfeiting

Counterfeiting is the production of 'fakes', that is, goods that, due to their design, trademark, logo, or company name, bear without authorization a reference to a brand, manufacturer, or organization as a warrant for the quality or standard conformity of the goods. Products that are vulnerable to counterfeiting can vary from highly visible, high volume, low-tech goods such as foodstuffs, alcohol, and tobacco to luxury products such as fashion goods to high-tech products such as pharmaceuticals, airplane parts, and car parts. Counterfeiting may lead to loss of sales for legal businesses, damages to brands (although occasionally companies may experience increased brand awareness as a result of counterfeiting), increased costs to legal businesses towards intellectual property protection, and, importantly, health and safety risks. In recent years, for example, hundreds of counterfeit aircraft microchips have been identified in the US defence supply chain, and in Oman 45 per cent of road fatalities in 2012 were attributed to counterfeit spare parts.

The World Trade Organization has an oft-repeated estimate of 7 per cent of all global commerce as counterfeit. The World Economic Forum goes further, suggesting that counterfeiting and piracy cost the global economy an estimated $1.77 trillion in 2015, or nearly 10 per cent of the global trade in merchandise. However, one needs to be cautious of these figures because of the illegal and, therefore, hidden nature of the activity. Estimates are most often based on seizures which give a partial indication of the scale of the phenomenon, but they also reflect the industry's tendency to magnify the problem.

There are several factors that facilitate counterfeiting. First, a huge demand such as this for luxury products at a significantly lower price, and public complicity. Second, outsourcing of production to developing countries towards reduced costs and entrusting cheap manufacturers with product designs. Third, the decentralization of the production phase in major counterfeit producing countries makes it impossible to cut off all production. Fourth, non-existent or inefficient legal frameworks of counterfeiting in many counterfeit production countries make the activity 'low-risk'. Moreover, the Internet and social media (Facebook, Twitter, etc.) constitute a 'convergence setting' for criminal entrepreneurs involved in various part of the supply chain products, and also facilitate the sales of various commodities to a much bigger and wider pool of customers internationally.

Counterfeits are produced primarily in developing countries such as China, Turkey, Thailand, India, Russia, and elsewhere. According to figures by the World Customs Organization, the US government and the European Commission, most of the world's counterfeit products originate from China. In 2009, China was the source of US\$205 million worth of counterfeit goods seized in the United States, a figure which amounts to 79 per cent of the value of all counterfeit products seized that year. In recent years, it has been observed that that production has moved to the Western world, too. The majority of companies producing branded products that are affected by counterfeiting are registered in the United States, France, Italy, Germany, Japan, Switzerland, Luxembourg, and the United Kingdom. Generally, the core of the counterfeit product supply chain comprises of counterfeit manufacturers, transporters, distributors, and retailers. A common and powerful perception is that the counterfeit market is primarily the business of Mafias around the world. Various national and international law enforcement agencies, industry bodies, and the UNODC have suggested that there are increasing links between counterfeiting of various commodities with arms trafficking, drug trafficking, human trafficking and smuggling, and money laundering. They also report involvement of rigidly structured organized crime groups such as the Russian Mafia, Chinese Triads, and Italian Mafia groups. Interestingly, counterfeiting has also been linked with terrorist and separatist groups in Northern Ireland, Spain, and Chechnya as well as with Hezbollah, Al-Qaeda, and ISIS that supposedly use the proceeds from the counterfeiting business to fund their other activities. Allegedly, even the North Korean regime has been involved in the counterfeiting and international distribution of cigarettes and currency.

Although these perceptions are partly true, they overlook very important aspects of the counterfeiting business, which are integral to an understanding of its characteristics and dynamics. Some actors may indeed be working for organized crime groups such as those mentioned in Chapter 2. Most participants in the business, however, are not always manipulated by 'organized criminals' as the official accounts suggest. They are often self-employed entrepreneurs. What may be viewed by some as criminal collaboration between a 'producer' and a seller does not necessarily involve an employer–employee relationship, but a business-to-business relationship. The counterfeit products market provides an employment refuge for a socially and economically excluded population, and most of the time there is no versatility in terms of the participants' activities.

Importantly, official and business analyses ignore critical studies on illegal markets highlighting the fact that counterfeiting is embedded in legal production and trade practices in a globalized economy. For example, a counterfeit product manufacturer most often obtains raw materials from a legitimate material supplier. Counterfeit schemes take advantage of the normal commercial channels, such as postage services or maritime shipping companies that transport containers to the biggest ports around the globe. For example, counterfeits enter Europe via major ports, which handle the biggest legal, commercial flows, such as Rotterdam (the Netherlands), Hamburg (Germany), Bremen (Germany), and Valencia (Spain), among others. Counterfeiters take advantage of trade hubs such as Hong Kong and Singapore as well as special economic zones such as the UAE, which guarantee the free flow of capital, lower taxes on imports and exports, and other 'business-friendly' conditions. Occasionally, there is also a mutually beneficial relationship between the legal and counterfeit products supply chains. There is, for instance, evidence that Italian organized criminals have been selling designer knock-offs manufactured by the same craftspeople who produce the originals.

Arms trafficking

According to the Small Arms Survey, in 2013 the illegal arms trade was worth more than US$1 billion and represented 10–20 per cent of the trade of legal arms. The illegal arms trade can be distinguished in a 'black' market which involves illegal transactions in all stages of the market; and a 'grey' market which involves large quantities of arms, some elements of authorized transactions, and the sale/distribution of arms to embargoed parties or countries. Generally, the illegality of the large-scale arms business is often a result of the quantity of arms produced and is subjected to international regulation, as well as a result of the false claims about the final use of the arms and their 'end user' and the destination of arms. For example, occasionally, the transfer of arms is disguised as humanitarian aid. In the 1990s, during the war in the former Yugoslavia, arms ended up going to the Muslim Bosnians as humanitarian aid from Arab countries.

Arms trafficking involves a diverse set of actors. When it comes to the large-scale, grey trade of arms, there is a variety of actors from the upperworld. First, arms manufacturers may be involved. Second, there are army officials, security services, and other governmental officials who are in close contact with the manufacturers and any stockpiles, since they monitor the production quantity and quality of arms. On rare occasions, army officials from rivalling armies can be involved in arms transactions. During the war in Yugoslavia, military units engaged in unconventional trading with the enemy, and on one occasion bargaining between a Serbian and a Muslim commander was monitored over the price of Serbian shells that the Muslim Bosnians wished to buy in order to fire at Croats. Third, there are brokers of sales, who act as links between buyers and sellers. Some of these brokers come from countries with large arms stockpiles and surpluses, and some from regions with stability problems. They tend to hold a number of passports and to be highly mobile, although many live in tax havens and other jurisdictions in which they are unlikely to be prosecuted. Finally, one can find politicians who are responsible for the transfer of arms, and it has been suggested that the arms black market has been a covert extension of diplomacy.

When it comes to the black market which involves smaller schemes, there are numerous ways in which arms can be procured. For example, legally held arms may be stolen. In 1997, after the collapse of the financial pyramid schemes in Albania and the resulting riots, army and police warehouses were raided, and thousands of assault rifles, hand grenades, and rounds of ammunition were stolen and diverted in illegal markets in various European countries. More recently, in February 2014 during the assaults on military units in Ukraine (a country which has been identified as a source of arms found in the Democratic Republic of Congo and South Sudan), radicals stole some 1,200 firearms, including around 1,000 Makarov handguns, over 170 Kalashnikov rifles, as well as machineguns and sniper rifles. Moreover, illicit firearms may be manufactured. In some areas, the unauthorized craft production of firearms by local gunsmiths is a significant source of illicit small arms. For instance, it has been reported that

Ghana's unlicensed gunsmiths have the capacity to produce up to 200,000 firearms of good quality in a year. Finally, it is not unusual, especially when it comes to small-scale, cross-border trafficking for arms to be bought from legal shops and gun shows. This is a common source of arms trafficking from the United States to Mexico, and the authorities believe that the major customers are the drug cartels.

A significant part of the black market is the terrain upon which individuals and groups unrelated to the arms manufacturers operate, such as the illicit manufacturers/gunsmiths mentioned earlier. In addition, traditional organized crime groups, such as outlaw motorcycle gangs in Australia, have been involved in and dominated the illegal trade of second-hand arms either regularly or on an ad hoc basis. As noted in Europol's latest Serious Organised Crime Threat Assessment (SOCTA) most of these groups enter the arms trafficking business through other criminal activities, which may offer contacts, knowledge of existing routes, and infrastructure related to the smuggling of arms. What is also interesting to note is that trafficking in firearms is most often reported to have been committed by citizens of the country in which the firearms were seized, followed by citizens of neighbouring countries.

Legitimate members of the public, illegitimate users such as criminals, insurgents, and terrorists, as well as armies, regular and irregular, constitute the buyers of illegally traded arms, each for different reasons, including for defence, display, direct use, value in use and display, kickback of the value of the deal, and so on. Occasionally, as mentioned earlier, embargoed states buy in the illegal market.

In several reported cases, traffickers used maritime services that typically transport containers through regular commercial channels. In most of those cases arms are concealed in other types of merchandise, and traffickers provide false or misleading information on the relevant shipping documents. In other cases, small arms were transported by commercial airlines and, in a small number of cases, even by post. In the trafficking of smaller quantities of small arms the schemes are rather simple. In many cross-border trafficking schemes, for example, long, porous, and inefficiently patrolled borders facilitate transportation by car, by truck, or even on foot. Prices of arms in the illegal market vary considerably depending among other factors upon the condition of the merchandise, local beliefs and perceptions about particular models, and their quality as well the stage of the conflict in which the transaction is made. Generally, arms prices in the black market increase in the early stages of a conflict. Illicit arms trafficking, especially of small arms, has been linked by the authorities with a variety of other manifestations of organized crime, and mainly with the trafficking of drugs and other commodities. In fact, there have been numerous historical examples internationally in which arms were traded for drugs, as in the case, for example, of the FARC rebels who provided cocaine in exchange for weapons for their cause; or diamonds exchanged for firearms in civil conflicts in Africa.

Extortion/protection

Extortion is the unlawful demand for money, property, behaviour, or other goods and services from another through the threat of force or actual force or harm to a person or property. In extortion, the threat of violence, actual violence, and their management are the commodities traded. Very often it is difficult to distinguish between extortion and protection, and this is why the two terms are often used interchangeably. Extortion implies a predatory activity in which there is a victim who receives very little in return, except protection from other extortionists. Criminal protection implies a genuine service and an agreement between two parties both receiving an advantage.

Extortion has been taking place in a variety of milieus from time immemorial. For many, it is the archetypal and defining activity of organized crime. It is an activity that targets primarily other criminals, since illegal enterprises cannot count on the state authorities for protection and for their right to be safeguarded. Indeed, illegal entrepreneurs have viewed extortion as an unavoidable 'informal tax' that is often 'legitimized' by the extortionists themselves. Extortion has been an entry-level activity for individuals embarking on professional crime careers or collectives of criminals attempting to establish a monopoly in an illegal market. Occasionally, traditional criminals extort their way into illegal entrepreneurial schemes (e.g. tobacco smuggling scheme) in something that could be described as a 'forced investment'.

Extortion has been present within immigrant communities, as they are generally unprotected by the authorities, and in which lack of trust of the authorities is pervasive. Extortion schemes have been the starting point and major activity for criminals from southern Italy who migrated in the United States in the end of the 19th century. A relevant scheme was also known as the 'Black Hand', which involved written demands of money primarily from Italian American businessmen, and threatened physical harm, destruction of property, or even death if the demands were not met. Similarly, in the 1990s, approximately 70 per cent of the Chinese-owned businesses in New York were subjected to extortion.

Generally, extortion is an activity that thrives in transitional societies, in which social arrangements are unclear and property rights are not easily enforced. Italian Mafias emerged as quasi-governmental institutions when the state was weak and failed to provide fair and sufficient protection of property rights, as was the case with the growth of market structures in the early 19th-century Italy. Intriguingly the Italian case can be compared with the emergence of violent entrepreneurial groups that often included law enforcement officers in post-Soviet Russia. These groups forced small and medium entrepreneurs to pay a protection fee (*krysha* or 'protective' roof) in order to avoid having their premises destroyed. The legalization of the protection service in 1992 in post-Soviet Russia, established a significant private security industry, which provided a range of services from private security to dispute settlement to debt collection, and created a framework within which the boundary between private security, protection, and extortion became blurred.

In a similar vein, violent entrepreneurs in Bulgaria have been an integral part of the organized crime scene in the country since the beginning of the 1990s. Being primarily sportsmen (weight lifters, wrestlers, boxers, martial artists, etc.), as well as former officers from intelligence and other agencies, and career criminals, violent entrepreneurs used and sold violence in their operations which included providing security for private companies and night-time economy establishments, debt collection, as well as mediation between businesses, before essentially capturing the insurance market.

In contemporary China, there has been a rise of extra-legal protection, a term referring to individuals or groups involved in private protection or quasi-law enforcement through violence or the abuse of official power. Organized crime groups re-emerged after the country adopted opening-up policies, economic reform, and market liberalization in 1978. This development has been understood to relate to the embeddedness of organized crime, corruption, and economic behaviour in social relations, specifically the *guanxi*. Such an understanding returns to the idea that when the state is weak, private individuals and entrepreneurs may turn to extra-legal actors for protection, and in the Chinese case such a stance arguably depends on existing *guanxi* networks with such actors.

Finally, extortion has been present in the workings of the legal economy. Traditionally, it may represent an expected business expense among many (legal) entrepreneurs in the nocturnal economy. Criminals with a violent reputation and capital have been used in the United States to break strikes, they often operated as mediators between employers and workers, and more often assisted in the suppression of the wage by controlling the labour union through violence and threat of violence. On the other hand, through the infiltration of the labour unions, criminals could extort businessmen by threatening strikes. There are more sophisticated extortion schemes through which criminals directly influence business decisions, for example, by setting up their own businesses selling goods and services to other businesses at inflated prices, or by placing associates in legal businesses to monitor and determine the optimal amount of money to be extorted. Researchers have also identified extortion schemes with an online element such as the threat of a denial-of-service attack to pornography and gambling websites. In these cases the perpetrators seek to make a machine or network resource unavailable to its intended users, if an extortion fee is not paid.

Generally, extortion affects local societies and their development; it promotes inefficiency and reduces competition; and affects the decision-making process of individuals and businesses as well as economies as a whole. The detection of and dealing with extortion depends on victims reporting their victimization to the authorities. Victims, however, are usually reluctant to do so—because their own activities are illegal; or because they distrust the authorities; or out of fear of retaliation by the extortionists.

Loansharking / illegal money lending

Loansharking is the lending of money at a high interest rate. The term usually refers to illegal/unlicensed money lending; however, it may also refer to extremely high interest lending by legal financial institutions, such as payday loan companies. Loansharking, which has been perceived as a typical organized criminal activity, has developed from the practice of salary lending in the 19th century, which involved money being loaned against future salaries at very high interest rates, and was a significant source of profit for many organized crime groups that emerged in the Prohibition era.

Loansharking becomes exacerbated in periods of financial hardship when there is a need for quick access to credit, and in this case some loan sharks tend to pool clients from poor estates, disadvantaged communities, and ethnic minority enclaves. Others lend money to legitimate business people who have financial problems. It has been estimated, for instance, that as many as 372,000 legal small businesses in Italy have borrowed money from a loan shark. Many illegal lenders 'specialize' in lending to gamblers. Illegal money lending has been viewed as an integral practice in casinos and other gambling premises. Loan sharks would take the burden off the casino management by lending to problem gamblers so that there would be no need for the casino to worry about collection. Loansharking is often seen as 'victimless' by the casino management. Often casino employees are involved in illegal lending practices. Some loan sharks offer loans to other criminals to start up a criminal enterprise or to sustain it.

Loan sharks are an extremely diverse group, and by no means is loansharking the monopoly of rigidly structured organized crime groups. There are two major types of loan sharks: the 'relatively benign' and the 'coercive' illegal lenders. Relatively benign illegal lenders consist of traditional informal money-lenders who lend small amounts of money within their immediate communities. The coercive group consists of three subtypes:

(a) The illegal lender operating a *stand-alone lending business*. These are highly profitable businesses and their profits are invested in legitimate assets such as properties. The lenders often run a quasi-legitimate business and/or a debt collection firm. In some countries, such as Bulgaria, organized crime groups exploit weaknesses in the national legislation to cover up illegal money lending schemes and to launder the proceeds through relevant legitimate business such as pawn shops and credit unions.

(b) The *retail model* in which lending is ancillary to sales of tax free alcohol, cigarettes, counterfeit goods, etc. In this model, loan sharks have illegal money lending as another item in their diverse portfolio including a range of legal and criminal entrepreneurial activities. The illegal lending sector is an important source of funds for a wide range of purposes. For example, it has been reported that paramilitary loyalist groups who operate within deprived communities in Northern Ireland have used illegal money lending services.

(c) The *criminal lifestyle model* in which lending is integrated with other forms of criminal activity. In this model, lenders who are involved criminal activities and markets recruit clients with payment difficulties into their criminal endeavours. For example, by using their houses or asking them to stash illegal goods.

The individual loan shark has limited funds to lend and tends to rely on peer or pester pressure to collect debts. In the loansharking business associated with an organized crime group, there are more funds available for the business and more resources to enforce the collection of a debt. Leaders of organized crime groups, who are the investors in the business and define the terms, usually isolate themselves from direct involvement in loansharking by delegating the activity to associate members. Money borrowed from the leader confirms the patron–client relationship.

Some illegal lenders pretend to act as legitimate lenders to lure people in need of financial support. Loan sharks often entrap the debtor in a continuous creditor–debtor relationship to generate an ongoing stream of income over an extended period of time. This obfuscates both the cost of the loan and the terms on which it is made, through a range of mechanisms. It has been found that the majority of clients of a Chinese loan shark in the Netherlands have taken out more than two loans. Loan sharks also maximize collection and reduce defaults by creating new loan opportunities. For example, they may reduce the interest of a client, grant a repayment extension, or even write off a part of the debt if the client introduces a potential client from his or her immediate social and business circle to the loan sharks. They also use deceptive techniques in convincing their clients to pawn significant collaterals, such as houses, cottages, business equipment, as well as company shares, with the intent of eventually acquiring the ownership. In cases that have been reported in Bulgaria, loan sharks participate in the debtors' legal and illegal businesses as investors. Enforcing a repayment schedule is integral to the loansharking business. There is a continuum of loan sharks' debt collection tactics. These may include 'polite' methods which involve, for example, the loan shark regularly visiting the debtor at his or her workplace. Loan sharks use violence as a secondary option, when they see it as being necessary for them to collect payments from debtors. Kidnap, torture, and rape also have been reported as collection tactics. Obtaining securities such as debtors' cash cards, pin numbers, or benefit books are important collection methods and allow the loan shark to have direct access to debtors' income streams. When loans are not repaid on time, some loan sharks impose a 'late fee' or re-possess some of the borrowers' necessary items (e.g. electrical appliances). When they realize that loans might not be repaid at all, they demand in-kind services such as cleaning homes and businesses, sexual favours, prostitution, or collaboration in criminal activities. Victims are reluctant to report loan shark activities to the authorities because loan sharks are often the only source of credit in a community; because of fear of reprisal; and, in the case of business people, because of the social stigma of being indebted to a loan shark and fear of losing business credibility.

Corporate crime

Corporate crime refers to crime committed by corporations or individuals acting on behalf of a corporation. It involves illegal

acts or omissions, which result from deliberate decision-making or culpable negligence within a legitimate organization.
Many corporate activities may be harmful but not necessarily illegal. It is not uncommon for these to be framed as accidents, particularly due to negligence. In fact, although some types of corporate activities are undoubtedly criminal, in numerous instances corporations have caused significant harm to the public, the environment, and the economy without having acted outside the law.

A 1980 study had found that 60 per cent of the US companies investigated had faced an average of four charges; 42 per cent of the companies in manufacturing had faced multiple charges—with the pharmaceutical, oil, and auto industries having the highest incidence of violations. Corporate criminality includes a wide range of activities of varying degrees of seriousness and impact. These may involve financial offences against employees, deceptive marketing practices, food crime (adulteration of food and food poisoning), crimes against consumers in general, the creation of oligopolies in markets and price fixing (competing companies agreeing not to sell below a certain price), industrial espionage, large-scale financial frauds, stock market manipulation, bribery of public officials, ignoring occupational health and safety, corporate manslaughter, as well as environmental crimes with devastating and long lasting results for communities around the globe. Perhaps the most notable example of corporate criminality of the latter kind is the explosion at the Union Carbide chemical plant in Bhopal (India) in December 1984. The incident resulted in the death of tens of thousands of people; while hundreds of thousands of people were injured (many thousands of them seriously); animals essential for the local populations died; and the soil and water in the wider area was contaminated. The destruction occurred because Union Carbide compromised health and safety regulations, and disregarded the law in order to maximize profit by operating a cheaper and dangerous plant in the developing world. It is not uncommon for corporations to be involved in more than one type of criminal activity. For instance, pharmaceutical corporations have been involved not only in unsafe manufacturing practices that are detrimental to the public's health, but also in a variety of financial manipulations and abuses.

Corporate crime possesses a number of distinct characteristics. Criminal activities take place within the confines of the corporation, providing relatively low visibility or complete invisibility. Moreover, these activities are based on at least some technical or specialized knowledge and expertise. For instance, large-scale financial fraud requires extensive knowledge of the financial markets. In addition, corporate criminal activities are usually the sum of actions or inactions of numerous individuals and departments within a corporation, resulting in a diffusion of the responsibility. Finally, most often there is no contact between the offenders and the victims, which occasionally may be other corporations.

There is an overlap between 'corporate crime' and 'organized crime' making it extremely difficult, if not impossible, to distinguish one from the other. It has been suggested that the two are variants of the same type or form of crime, and as such they should be analysed jointly. In many cases there is infiltration of the legitimate business by organized crime, which ranges from a complete 'take over' to a symbiosis between crime-enterprises and legitimate corporations. For example, in 'long-firm' fraud schemes a trading company is established for fraudulent purposes. In some cases, the ways legitimate corporations operate justify this joint analysis. For instance, in many European countries, legally registered industrial waste processing companies run their own parallel illegal schemes with the choice between the two services depending on what the customers can afford or are willing to pay. There is evidence to suggest that from the late 1980s and up until the beginning of the 2000s legal tobacco manufacturers were involved in the smuggling of billions of packs of their own brands. Gallagher, BAT, Philip Morris, and RJ Reynolds were major actors in the illicit tobacco business in the UK and abroad. They created an illegal market for their own brand of cigarettes in the UK by facilitating the exportation of cigarettes and then re-importing them into the UK.

It is difficult to offer an account of the scale of corporate crime for several reasons. First, very often victims of corporate crime are simply not aware of their victimization. An individual's loss may be insubstantial. Second, the victimization is often temporally distant from corporate criminality. The effects of the criminal activity may even take years to become apparent, and the victims may not be able to make a connection between their victimization and a particular corporate activity. Third, once victims become aware of their victimization, they do not know where to report it. The authorities that deal with corporate crime are not always known to members of the public. Fourth, many victims prefer to deal with the issue privately. Finally, many victims feel ashamed of their victimization and avoid discussing the issue altogether. This is especially the case with forms of financial crime committed by corporations. Although it is difficult to accurately measure the impact of corporate crime, it has been suggested that females, children, the elderly, and the poorer segments of the population are disproportionally affected.

Despite the huge costs of corporate crime, it is dealt with rather leniently by the authorities. The levels of inspection and detection are low, and most often corporate criminal offenders are not prosecuted. The reason for the poor prosecution rate of corporations is a result of the difficulty of proving liability; offshore accounts in which proceeds of crime are hidden; the diffusion of responsibility, which is an important feature of corporate criminality, especially when multinational corporations are concerned; lobbying on the part of corporations as well as the use of other resources by corporate criminals. When corporations pay fines, in the vast majority of cases these are extremely low compared to the harms and damages caused, and as such they are hardly a deterrent. For example, in 1983, almost 10 tons of oil was spilled into Botany Bay (near Sydney) from an Australian oil refinery pipeline, the fifth spillage by that company in seven years. The fine imposed was only AU$300.

Money laundering

Money laundering is the process which obscures the link between the proceeds of crime, tax evasion, and corruption, and the original activity, and transforms these proceeds to legitimate assets. Money laundering is associated with all types of profit-driven crime, and is considered a part of the 'logistics of organized crime'. Estimates suggest that the amount of money that is laundered are close to US$1.6 trillion or 2.7 per cent of global GDP. However, this estimate, just as previous estimates that have been offered as justification for the creation of an international anti-money laundering regime, has been criticized for the possible invalidity of the data used, and has been considered simply to be an 'informed guess' that has only gained some reliability through repetition.

There are three stages in the money laundering process: a) the *placement* of funds from its original source and its introduction in the financial system; b) *layering*, that is, the disguising of the provenance of funds by means of further transactions or conversions; and c) *integration*, which is the re-introduction of the 'clean' funds into the legal economy. This, however, is a simplified description of the process. Some transactions may involve more than these three stages, specifically, the *justification* of crime money and the *embedding* of crime money into the (legal) economy. Very often the stages overlap. Moreover, in the case of financial crime which involves funds that are already in the (legal) financial system (e.g. fraud), placement is not required.

Money laundering is the platform for an extremely diverse set of schemes of varying sophistication and actors. Schemes may involve simple cash deposits of relatively small amounts that do not attract attention (also known as 'smurfing'); small cash deposits in numerous bank accounts often in neighbouring countries; or the physical transportation/smuggling of cash out of the country to jurisdictions with less diligent or rigorous enforcement of anti-money laundering procedures. It has been suggested that in early 2016, 20 per cent of all Euro banknotes in denominations from €50 to €500 were not in circulation in Europe, raising the suspicion that they were used by criminals, tax evaders, and money launderers, who preferred them because of their ease of transportation relative to their value. Other laundering schemes may involve methods such as phoney bookkeeping in cash-intensive, retail service businesses to allow crime money to be mixed with the cash flow of the legitimate business; buying transportable, high value commodities such as diamonds, art (Box 3), and real estate; or the unwitting participation of a bank through the provision of 'normal' services to clients. In some jurisdictions, such as Russia, criminals established their own banks in their 1990s to manage their finances and launder money from other illicit activities.

Gambling and betting establishments have been employed by criminals to launder 'dirty' money. Moreover, money remittance providers, such as Western Union or MoneyGram, and foreign exchange bureaus have also been regularly used in the process. The Financial Action Task Force (FATF), an intergovernmental body that oversees the anti-money laundering regime, reports numerous cases in which remittance services and currency exchange businesses have been knowingly as well as unwittingly involved in money laundering associated with drug trafficking, human trafficking, fraud, and financial crimes. A case from the Dutch Financial Intelligence Unit revealed that three women traffickers from Nigeria sent money to their country from the Netherlands more than 600 times, making up a total value of approximately €120,000. Similarly, informal money transfer systems, which are not necessarily criminal in nature (but are

Box 3 Laundering money through art in Greece

One of the main methods of laundering significant proceeds of crime and corruption in the late 1990s and 2000s in Greece involved the *virtual transactions* between individuals who owned paintings (and who wished to launder dirty money) and a gallerist/collector of pieces of art in Athens, who was also a stockbroker. The process was as follows. The gallerist/collector would appear to buy a painting from a person interested in laundering dirty money. He or she would sign a contract and the 'seller' would sign an unofficial declaration that he or she had received a named amount from the gallerist, which would constitute the proof of laundering of money that could not otherwise have been justified within the 'seller's' asset and funds-source declaration to the tax authorities. The unofficial declaration would read:

> I [name of seller] sell and deliver this painting to the collector [name of collector] for the amount of [€XXX,XXX], which is considered a fair amount and corresponds to the value of the painting, and which was paid to me today in whole in cash.

The gallerist would receive a commission for his or her services, which corresponded to 10 per cent of the supposed value of the painting (i.e. the amount that was essentially laundered). In two of the virtual transactions that came to light, the amounts laundered were €115,000 and €260,000. Money laundering through art was particularly popular with corrupt Greek tax officials, ministry employees, and other public officials who could not justify their income.

known as 'underground banking') have been exploited. Examples of such systems are the *hawala*, a traditional system in Arab and South Asian countries by which legitimate remittances from diasporic communities are routinely transferred, or the *fei ch'ien* ('flying money'), the Chinese underground banking system.

In some occasions *trade-based* money laundering is conducted, which is the process of disguising the proceeds of crime and moving value using trade transactions through, for example, over-valuing or under-valuing invoices.

Money laundering schemes may involve more complicated and sophisticated methods such as offshore banking, and the use of shell companies registered in tax havens such as the Cayman Islands, Seychelles, and Delaware (United States), among many others, to make tracing funds to criminal activities difficult, if not impossible (see Box 4). It is not uncommon, of course, for combinations of the above methods to be employed.

Many profit-driven criminals are financially unsophisticated individuals, who most often do not have the capacity to launder their crime money themselves due to the ever tightening anti-money laundering regime. Rather, they look for the services of formal and informal service providers to circumvent anti-money laundering procedures. These money laundering facilitators are not typical criminals, and have a different criminal career to those in property or violent crime. With some exceptions, such as cash couriers or smugglers, these facilitators are embedded in the legitimate sector. They seem to be involved with organized crime at a later stage of their professional career, when they are asked to provide their expertise. A significant number of money laundering services are opportunistic, although there are facilitators who work on a continuous basis with organized criminals especially those are embedded in the 'upperworld'. These facilitators may be insiders from the banking system. For instance, a bank employee may be forced or bribed to facilitate a suspicious transaction without notifying the authorities. Foreign currency exchangers, financial services company employees, 'underground bankers', art dealers, car dealers, dealers in high value commodities, real estate agents, casino employees, insurance brokers, stockbrokers, notaries, accountants, and lawyers have also been integral to the laundering process.

Box 4 Setting up a shell company in a tax haven

In 2016, the world was shaken by the leak of more than eleven million documents from Mossack Fonseca, a Panama-based law firm which specialized in setting up offshore companies in financial havens around the globe that would guarantee the anonymity of asset holders. Following the leak, *Financial Times* journalist, Michael Stothard, attempted to set up his own offshore companies to see what the process involved. With the help of a sales assistant working for a UK-based business management consultants' company, he initially bought a shell company in Seychelles. Setting up the company, which he named Pirate's Chest, cost £335; there were no residency requirements; no obligation to fill annual accounts; no tax; and guaranteed confidentiality. Ownership was masked by 'nominee directors' who although controlling the company on paper, had no decision-making powers and did not have any active part in the company. Stothard also bought another company in Delaware, named Stuffed Parrot, which on paper was owned by his Seychelles company. This 'layering' of companies, which is a popular practice in the money laundering business, confuses law enforcement with regards to ownership, and according to the journalist, rich Russians own as many as twenty or thirty shell companies with a single asset to make the trail of dirty money disappear. A court case is needed to investigate and identify the beneficiary of each shell company, which is a time-consuming and costly process and may even then show no results.

However, it should be mentioned that organized criminals, and others who wish to 'clean' their money, are not a homogeneous group. Official data on asset confiscation shows that although a large amount of (organized) crime money exists, its distribution is unequal. Basically, this means that many will possess a small part of each criminal market with modest profits that simply spill over into the legal economy through lifestyle spending, for example on expensive clothes, watches, food and alcohol, holidays, and so on; or small investments in legal businesses of family or friends. The decentralized nature of organized crime creates an environment in which crime money is widely distributed rather than retained in the hands of a few, and as such money laundering is not always necessary to the process.

Chapter 4
Controlling and preventing organized crime

In Chapters 2 and 3, we considered organized crime from the viewpoint of the various contexts in which criminal groups operate; and of the activities in which they are likely to engage. This chapter offers a discussion of policies and approaches towards the control and prevention of organized crime. To view organized crime from the perspective of policymaking, law enforcement, and justice administration is not simply about tackling organized crime. Policy decisions, legislative frameworks, police actions, and the judicial process influence directly how the issue is defined, debated, and experienced in society. For example, the Sicilian Mafia existed in Italy long before the word *Mafia* became synonymous with 'organized crime' in the 1950s in the United States. In the 1920s and 1930s, the Italian government of Benito Mussolini perceived the Mafia as a challenge to the political authority of the state, and engaged in a campaign to eradicate it for this reason. The ways we understand organized crime today very much depend on the ways institutions think and act about it.

The politics of organized crime control

The idea of the Mafia as an ethnic-based criminal organization possessing a hierarchy, a specific set of positions, and ruthless internal discipline has heavily influenced the legislative, investigative, and prosecutorial strategies of the United States. As early as 1951, the Mafia was identified by the special US Senate Kefauver Committee as a 'sinister' syndicate of such criminal organizations or 'families' specializing in drugs, gambling enterprises, prostitution, and interference with legitimate businesses using extortion and violence. The 1967 President's Commission report on organized crime consolidated the idea of organized crime as a conspiracy, posing a threat to both society (by means of supplying illegal goods and services and interfering with legitimate business) and government (by means of corruption of officials and interference with the political process). In addressing the question of organized crime, the United States in the late 1960s not only possessed experience in investigative methods that dated as far back as the Prohibition era, but also became equipped with a specific concept of the phenomenon.

The significance of this development is that the United States became the first country to develop a comprehensive and wide-ranging response to the phenomenon it identified as 'organized crime'. Specific prohibitions involving drug and other offences, criminal conspiracy, and tax evasion laws, as well as investigative techniques, such as the use of eavesdropping devices to gather information and evidence, had been used for a long time to penetrate the secrecy and to target the activities of organized criminals. Legislation introduced at the end of the 1960s gave prosecutors a new model based on patterns of criminal activity rather than on specific offences. Alongside the new tools for developing cases against criminal groups, it increased the severity of sanctions in such cases. Responses against organized crime that are standard today, such as criminal asset seizure and forfeiture or anti-money laundering regulations, took a robust form during that era. This legislative wave also formalized the use of more intrusive investigative techniques and brought about a new enhanced operational role and capacity for US federal law enforcement agencies.

The US lead in organized crime control was consequential beyond its national borders. Its justice and law enforcement agencies accumulated significant experience in implementing a framework that the US government could then herald internationally as a model response. This must be seen in the light of the position of the United States in international politics, and of its decision to move the defence line against organized crime abroad. Drug markets, which the Mafia was perceived to control, became an important vehicle for the internationalization of the American approach and the activity of law enforcement agencies. President Richard Nixon's 'war on drugs' entailed a scaling up of US federal law enforcement agencies in their international presence and interactions with their counterparts abroad. They disseminated their ideas and practices in organized crime control, and advocated for the development of frameworks of international cooperation that ultimately meant that other countries had to converge with the US model.

The routinization of US practices and exercise of influence internationally has amounted to something described as an 'Americanization' of organized crime control policies across a range of countries, including European countries, which differed from the US both in their experience and perception of the issue, and in terms of their legal traditions. Arguably the US influence has led a trend towards more aggressive and intrusive law enforcement approaches using intelligence and surveillance, and towards substantive and procedural legal reform, with a view to securing convictions and imposing severe sanctions. The model also encourages a move towards more centralized institutional designs, nationally and internationally. Europol, the policing agency of the European Union was seen in the early 1990s as a 'European FBI'; and, similarly, the UK's National Crime Agency is often viewed as an FBI-style agency.

The perception of organized crime as an international issue, indeed as an issue of international security, has not only added to the above dynamic, but it also enabled new actors to emerge and play a role in orchestrating policy developments 'from above'. For example, with anti-money laundering having become a key component of the organized crime control model, a new intergovernmental body, the FATF (see also Chapter 3) was established in 1989 by the G-7 s, the European Commission, and eight other countries. The purpose of the FATF is to set standards and encourage the development of legislation, measures, and techniques to suppress money laundering globally. FATF is not an international organization, meaning it has no legal standing in any country, but it does monitor developments in financial crime, and the progress of legislative and regulatory reforms relative to this area.

Established international actors, such as the United Nations, more expectedly became increasingly involved in the development of the international organized crime control regime in the 1990s and thereafter. An important landmark has been the conclusion of the United Nations Convention against Transnational Organized Crime (UNTOC) in 2000. Generally referred to as the Palermo Convention, due to the international conference that took place in the city for the opening for signature, it entered into force in 2003 and it is the main international instrument against transnational organized crime. The convention is supplemented by three protocols, which address manifestations of organized crime: human trafficking, human smuggling, and the illegal manufacturing and trade in firearms and ammunition. The countries party to the convention, currently 187, commit themselves to a series of measures against transnational organized crime. These include the identification of criminal offences, in other words the participation in an organized criminal group; money laundering; corruption and obstruction of justice; the adoption of new and sweeping frameworks for extradition; mutual legal assistance; law enforcement cooperation; and the promotion of training and technical assistance for building or upgrading the necessary capacity of individual national authorities. Necessarily, international conventions involve a 'minimum common denominator' approach between the negotiating parties. As a result, evaluating the uniformity and pace of the implementation as well as the concrete impact of the UNTOC has proven to be a challenging exercise, from both a political and a practical viewpoint. There is no doubt, however, that, at the level of policy principles, the provisions of the UNTOC amount to a comprehensive and unprecedented platform for the development of international cooperation against organized crime.

In Europe, the combination of the acceleration of the project of integration among the member states of the European Union and the tremendous geopolitical change experienced in Eastern Europe opened up a unique field for the growth of organized crime control policies. Historically, the manifestations of and approaches towards the phenomena labelled as organized crime have varied across European countries. The recognition of the issue has not been met without scepticism or resistance among legal and scholarly communities in individual European countries. A conceptualization, however, along the prevailing lines of hierarchical structures with potential for control, corruption, and cross-border activity has provided a suitable enemy. Organized crime has been perceived to be bolstered by the development of the EU's internal market and the lifting of internal EU border checks on one hand, and the conditions of economic and social turmoil in the transitioning Eastern European countries on the other. It was increasingly seen as a threat to economic, social, and political life and institutions, conducive to the development of the EU's internal security agenda.

As a result, European institutions have been able to engage in the development of extensive infrastructure, including dedicated agencies to support police and judicial cooperation, such as Europol and Eurojust. Closely interwoven with the evolution of the European 'constitutional' framework has been the promulgation of related programmes and policies explicitly addressing organized crime. These on the one hand have involved practical cooperation and technical assistance, as for example the introduction of joint investigative teams and of the European Arrest Warrant. On the other, EU institutions have played a leading role in the harmonization and approximation of the EU member states legislation. An important moment in the process has been the European Council's Framework Decision on the fight against organized crime. This provides a definition of organized crime as a 'structured association' and requires member states to take the necessary measures to ensure the criminalization of those relating to the 'aim and general activity of the criminal organization'. European institutions have also intervened actively in energizing cooperation and harmonization relating to activities or aspects organized crime, such as human trafficking or money laundering.

Despite the wishes of academic and practitioner communities, approaches to organized crime and its control are not a merely technical matter, and they always involve a political agenda and content. In the People's Republic of China, for example, organized crime is defined narrowly along the lines of the hierarchical structure paradigm (even though there is considerable variation in the forms criminal groups may take), organized crime control appears to be significantly influenced by the evolving relations between central government and local authorities in the context of increasing economic liberalization. The central state has waged significant campaigns against 'organized crime' to target local enforcement laxity and corruption, and to pre-empt local institutions' potential weakening of political control.

Responses to organized crime: law, practice, and prevention

Organized crime poses some special problems for law enforcement and judicial authorities mandated to contain and suppress it. Often occurring in clandestine conditions, large or important parts of the activity it involves may be less visible or entirely hidden from view. Similarly, important actors that coordinate the activity or benefit from it may do so while remaining at a distance from the parts of the activity that may more readily be identified as one of the typical predatory or violent offences punished by law. In those cases, even when arrests can be made and convictions can be secured, the effective suppression of the criminal activity may remain doubtful. The multitude of actors involved may mean that individuals are expendable or replaceable, since the essence of organized crime lies with the activity itself. Ever since it emerged as an issue and social threat, organized crime has offered legislators, and law enforcement and judicial authorities, a field for innovation. Al Capone, the notorious gangster of the US Prohibition era, remained elusive to conventional criminal law despite maintaining a highly public profile. He was prosecuted and convicted for tax offences. In other examples, main figures of organized crime have been brought to justice on charges not directly related to the core of their business.

While the exigencies of addressing organized crime inevitably call for a re-assessment and fuller mobilization of available institutional armouries in various contexts, it is not difficult to see that they inevitably engender a specific dynamic for an intensification or expansion of criminal law. One possible response may be that the criminal sanctions for traditional crime typically associated with organized crime are made more severe, for example by raising the lower limits of prison sentences prescribed by the law in these cases. Another path would involve the introduction of new statutes, or the revision of existing ones, criminalizing specific types of conduct so as to target more effectively the range of activities associated with organized crime. Drug prohibitions, for example, can be extended to target a wider range of: precursor substances; stages in the production of illegal drugs; or quantities of illegal drugs that are made available for sale. Such responses, however, do not necessarily suffice in stopping a given criminal activity, for reasons explained earlier.

From the viewpoint of crime control policy, the strategic aim is to suppress the criminal activity in its entirety, or at least to a meaningful extent, making it very difficult or less profitable for criminal groups to continue engaging in it.

Seizure and forfeiture of the means used in, or to facilitate, the criminal activity or of the proceeds derived from it are measures aimed at disrupting the activity of organized crime. Forfeiture may follow a conviction for a criminal offence or it may take place at an earlier stage, for example when smuggled goods are intercepted and then confiscated by the authorities. It can extend to any type of asset as long as a link with criminal activity can be established. An example of how targeting the means or proceeds of organized crime can be integrated in criminal law responses can be found in anti-money laundering legislation. Such laws typically involve a monitoring system by introducing an obligation of financial institutions to report to financial intelligence units (FIUs) transactions that are deemed suspicious. If the existence of a money laundering scheme can be detected in the investigation that may ensue, then forfeiture may target the funds and the other assets whose acquisition can be linked to that particular dirty money. This approach is intended not only to reduce the appeal of illicit financial gain, but also to disrupt the use of such funds for the continuation of criminal activity, and to prevent organized crime from infiltrating and corrupting the legitimate economy.

The intensification and expansion of criminal law in the context of organized crime control can be clearly seen in the effort to identify the wider group of individuals involved in any criminal activity. Although there is variation among jurisdictions, two main approaches can be distinguished. The first, reflecting a conspiracy model drawn from common law jurisdictions, requires an agreement of two or more persons to commit a crime. The agreement itself constitutes an offence separate from the committed crime. An organized crime scheme can be captured by the conspiracy model even when those involved in a scheme do not interact directly with each other but are aware of the overall activity. The second model is that of criminal association, according to which any conduct associated with a criminal activity is criminalized. The circle of participants can be drawn very widely. The 2000 UN convention, for example, requires state parties to establish as criminal offences the 'organising, directing, aiding, abetting, facilitating or counselling the commission of serious crime involving an organised criminal group'. This approach may extend the circle of individuals deemed to be associated with the criminal activity well beyond the group directly involved in the commission of the particular crimes.

A distinctive approach that overcomes the limitations of the conspiracy and association models, which involve the elements of agreement and involvement respectively, is found in the US Racketeer Influenced and Corrupt Organizations statute of 1970, commonly known as RICO. This model targets 'enterprise' criminality in the sense that it aims to capture those involved in the more complex forms of conduct associated with organized crime. Racketeering activity in the RICO sense is associated with a range of named offences (18 US Code §1961), deemed to be symptomatic of organized crime. When two or more of these crimes are committed within a period prescribed by the law, and a relation or continuity between them can be established, they constitute a pattern of racketeering activity. RICO criminalizes three types of conduct, namely (a) the use or investment of funds derived from racketeering activity to establish an enterprise (or the acquisition of an interest in an existing one); (b) the gaining or maintaining control of any enterprise through a pattern of racketeering activity; and (c) the operation of an enterprise through a pattern of racketeering activity. While RICO has not been readily transferable to other countries, within the US context it has proved to be a very flexible and successful tool in combating organized crime, because its structure covers a wide variety of situations.

The push towards organized crime control has also created the need for bolder and more novel approaches to law enforcement. In the context of crime investigation, drug enforcement has provided a template since the techniques used to penetrate the clandestine circuits of the production, supply, and trade of illicit drugs have been applied to other forms of organized crime activity. The over-arching theme in organized crime control approaches is proactivity, since, unlike the investigation of conventional crime, organized crime cases require organization, planning, and analytical work to build on initial suspicion or partial information. The investigation of organized crime depends heavily on the gathering of information. Collated and analysed information can be used either to build specific cases with a view to securing successful prosecutions and convictions, or, as intelligence, to provide an overview of the nature, patterns, and specific aspects of organized crime. The proactive character of organized crime control on the basis of intelligence is underscored by the development of early warning systems regarding risks in existing or emergent areas of activity. The EU SOCTA (see also Chapter 3), which is produced by Europol and involves a detailed analysis of the threat of serious and organized crime facing the EU, is an example of this trend.

While traditional techniques are relevant, there are certain practices relating to the collection of information which appear to be characteristic of organized crime investigation. Overt or covert surveillance of individuals, locations, and activity is one traditional technique, which the development of technological means has brought to new qualitative levels. Means such as recording equipment or tracking devices allow law enforcement agents to remain invisible in surveillance operations. Equally, the development of digital technologies, including sophisticated software, allows investigators to track or intercept communication flows via telephone or the Internet. The providers of communication services to the public can be required to assist investigations undertaken in this way when certain conditions are met as prescribed by the law.

A different route to information gathering in organized crime investigation involves the use of informants. This is again a technique historically associated with other forms of police activity, but it is of particular relevance in organized crime investigation. Informants are individuals selected to provide information to law enforcement agents due to their proximity or even participation in a criminal activity. A more drastic approach involves the infiltration of criminal groups by undercover police agents, who can be involved in the activities of those groups for a short or longer period of time.

Information gathering operations raise serious dilemmas in terms of policy and practice, since, on the one hand, they may be highly intrusive and detrimental to privacy, and on the other, they may involve considerable risk to the law enforcement personnel involved. Furthermore, information gathering itself raises concerns about access to and the sharing of information. As the storing and transferring of information has been moving from physical to digital formats, such concerns have naturally become more pronounced.

Organized crime control does not develop in the context of criminal law enforcement alone. The complexity of its object calls for more complex approaches involving a range of agencies beyond criminal law enforcement and the criminal justice system. An idea that has become increasingly popular builds on the idea that organized crime does not operate in a vacuum, and it is therefore likely to be subject to a variety of administrative laws and regulations that any legitimate activity and business must complies with. Administrative approaches fall in the space between the disruption, suppression, and prevention of organized crime. Registration or licensing systems for the catering and hospitality industry; legislation and regulations regarding tax and access to public subsidies or facilities; regulations for public order disturbances; and also the system of administrative sanctions relating to such regulations can be used to disrupt the business of organized crime, particularly at the local level. A typical example of an administrative approach is the screening for prior criminal activities of persons or legal entities applying for a permit or licence for an activity—to operate, for example, a bar or a restaurant. If the applicant fails to satisfy set criteria, through which the nature of the legitimate activity can be related to illicit activity, the application is refused.

At this point, readers will have noticed that most of the discussion about addressing the issue of organized crime is concerned with the ways and means to react against it. Enhancing the reach and effectiveness of investigation or aiding the securing of convictions follows the actual occurrence of the criminal activity. Yet an obvious question is, can this activity be prevented?

An idea that has enjoyed some popularity among policy and scholarly circles is that organized crime could be prevented situationally. Situational crime prevention rests on the assumption that crime essentially builds on a cost-benefit calculation on the part of the offender. Once an opportunity has been recognized, the crime involves the convergence in time and space of any such motivated offender and a suitable victim without capable 'guardians'. It follows that prevention entails an intervention to manipulate the parameters of that cost-benefit calculation so as to reduce or eliminate the appeal of this opportunity, for example by increasing the effort required in committing that crime; or increasing the risk of exposure to law enforcement agencies; or reducing the rewards of the criminal activity.

While the situational crime prevention approach to organized crime would intuitively appeal to many, closer reflection suggests that the diversity of the activities of criminal groups would entail a detailed examination of their business and modus operandi, so that the measures leading to opportunity reduction or 'target-hardening' can be identified. At the same time, group activity differs significantly from the lone-offender exemplar on which situational crime prevention typically rests. As an activity, organized crime is distinguished by its durability, which itself relates closely with the social and economic conditions under which it unfolds. In other words, organized crime groups relate meaningfully with the social reality that surrounds them and often actively manipulate it. The object of organized crime is a far cry from the static target to be situationally protected from a lone operator, like a car to be stolen or a property to be burgled. Ultimately, because the disruption of organized crime is the disruption of a business, too much target-hardening could possibly interfere with the conduct of legitimate economic activity as well—for example, by placing too many controls on every day, routine financial transactions that organized crime may latch onto.

One final word is necessary here about a dimension that is often missing from discussions of organized crime. As we have seen, the preponderant concern is about measures and actions to suppress it. Considerations of what motivates those involved in it, and of the social and economic conditions that define their situation and prompt them to engage in these patterns of activity take second place, if any place at all. The ebb and flow of organized crime may well depend on wider economic and social conditions, from the decline of the industries that criminal groups were once able to interfere with but not anymore, to the changing nature of local politics. The persistence of organized crime may be pointing to the substantive problems that underpin it as an activity or a set of activities. Poverty, blocked opportunity, and the inability to fulfil the ambitions and desires that the prevailing culture imposes can be such substantive problems and strong motivators for both those who are involved in it as well as their clients.

Chapter 5
Business as usual

Our aim in this final chapter is to bring together and evaluate
the different images of organized crime that we have considered
so far. We began by alerting our readers to the many serious
difficulties raised by the concept or idea of organized crime. There
is something frustrating about the lack of a clear-cut path to
achieving satisfactory levels of conceptual clarity and certainty
about organized crime. The exploration of such a path, however, is
not simply a scientific endeavour that can be pursued with the
precision of a natural science in laboratory-like conditions. The
idea that organized crime is a socially constructed phenomenon
reflects the reality that a variety of institutions and everyday life
experience, and views of this experience, are an inherent part of
the process of defining and addressing it. Crime is a scandalizing
and fascinating issue, because in every one of us it strikes some
very sensitive chords about the nature and outlook of our social
life, order, and security. Inevitably, thinking about crime, and
knowing what it is, depends on a complex process that has to do
with the ways members of the public and institutions are
sensitized towards it and develop responses to address it. Media
representations and political agendas may energize this process in
the first place, and also, typically, feed back and capitalize on it.

The application of the label 'organized crime' has at its early stage
depended heavily on moralizing campaigns and visions of social

engineering that generated many of the prohibitions responsible for the growth of the phenomena associated with it. Some of the phenomena themselves, the human and social activity involved, had a history that long preceded the label, and in many cases the prohibitions. The social scientists involved in the study of organized crime did not come up with the idea, but rather met with it at a given stage of its career. The process of social research often requires us to deal with what members of the public and institutions take for granted, a situation that influences both what evidence is available or can be produced, and what can be made of it. The initial understanding of 'organized' crime with reference to hierarchical organizations featuring a robust division of labour and strict rules about membership built on widely publicized and sensational, but rather limited, evidence about the Italian-American Mafia. The meteoric rise of the question of 'transnational organized crime' in the 1990s parallels the dominance of the Mafia framework in the mid-20th century. The 'alien conspiracy' theory of organized crime may have reflected the much wider attraction of notions building on a 'conspiracy of suitable enemies' into which anxieties and perceptions of threat are often channelled.

Students of organized crime are not unfamiliar with the realization that institutions may conform with prevailing notions so as to boost the credibility of their activity. They often come across the phenomenon of 'facts by repetition', which refers to the circulation of estimates (perhaps 'guesstimates') about the turnover, gains, or victims of an organized crime business. Such realities not only reinforce the dominant viewpoint but also underscore the fact that scientific research necessarily converses with the wider social context in which it takes place. The official and popular image of organized crime was almost immediately challenged in the early 1970s and afterwards by the social scientific research triggered by the gravity of the issues and its implications. There is today a significant evidence base showing that the structure of organized crime can be very diverse, and that, in fact, organized crime is *not* very well organized. Compiling this alternative image has required conceptual and methodological creativity and innovation, and, in many cases, practical risks. Rich and solid data from official sources are not, with some notable exceptions, always accessible or available, and the organizations dealing with organized crime or aspects of it are often reluctant to work with researchers. The emergence of the alternative idea that much organized crime involves loose and opportunistic associations or networks of offenders typically requires researchers to gain access to obscure populations and fluid domains of social activity that often extends across borders.

The suggestion that an understanding of organized crime may be better facilitated by means of particular analytical entry points rather than a definition, which at any rate appears impossible given the state of play in the field, reflects both the advances made and the difficulties involved in the study of organized crime. From our necessarily brief overview of the various forms and activities of organized crime, it emerges that these analytical entry points, structure, activity, and extra-legal governances, are useful, but not always equally pertinent. Undoubtedly, organized crime often requires a technical division of labour which corresponds to the various phases of a process each time. This characteristic may apply within the specific domains of criminal activity, such as the trade of drugs or human smuggling and trafficking. It may also be present in the co-articulation of activities as a process, for example, in the laundering of the money gained from the illicit trade. The consideration of the process of organized crime also suggests that a social division of labour may also be present, since the activity may require interaction and complicity between illicit and legitimate actors. When one part of the process takes place at social margins where actors strive to secure an income, and another part in the 'upperworld', where entrepreneurs seek to expand their business, the social distance between the actors can be construed as a hierarchy, but it is not, or it is not necessarily, a hierarchy of the employer–employee kind that one encounters in formal organizations. This is not to say that hierarchical relations in the organization of an illicit trade do not exist. For example, evidence from the Netherlands showed that in the 1990s the cocaine trade was directly managed from Colombia, and Colombian supervisors enforced discipline on the ethnically diverse lower executives. Yet, even in this case it would be difficult to speak of a Mafia-type hierarchy.

In other cases, the outlook of the activity has the consequence of affirming existing social hierarchies of the patron–client type found in more traditionalist societies. The fact, for example, that ethnic Turkish groups have featured highly in the trade of heroin in Western Europe is directly related with Turkey's geographical position, which gives this country a prominent place in that trade. It is rather unsurprising that kinship connections influence considerably the outlook of the supply line and trade, just as lines of authority follow the organization of family relations centring on senior members of the family. On the other hand, even in such cases, the openness of the market ultimately dilutes the ethnic element, which has been understood to reinforce the internal discipline of Mafia-type organizations. Historically, researchers and investigators have encountered difficulties affirming the ethnic homogeneity even in the archetypal case of Italian-American organized crime. More generally speaking, how authority is constituted in a given society appears to play a role in the outlook and activity of any organized crime within it. The survival of traditionalist social relations and weak state political controls and law enforcement encourage and sustain political parasitism and economic predation by organized crime.

When one considers the openness, fluidity, and opportunism that characterize illicit markets and which dictate the forms of participation and association actors may adopt in them, the intensive and sustained mobilization of states and international institutions and the fury of activity in the issue area is astounding. Within a period of approximately fifty years a formidable institutional, legislative, and investigative armoury has been constructed and has proliferated internationally to address the threat of organized crime. As we have seen, this development has not only involved the modernization of pre-existing criminal law and criminal law enforcement approaches and techniques, it has also included an outright expansion of the capacity of authorities to regulate the ways rights and liberties are exercised and to reach into the private life of citizens. It has been suggested that (transnational) organized crime is a new form of authoritarianism that affects all aspects of economic, social, and political life, and that its wealth and power potentially undermines 'even the strongest democracies'. The question is whether such a description is accurate and whether such a counter-mobilization is commensurate with the overall status of the problem. It is true that as regards particular contexts (e.g. Mexico, where the effects of drug cartel wars have been devastating; or Eastern European migrations, in the course of which a great number of women have become prey to sexual exploitation in the West and elsewhere), the situation and its suggested response does not seem over-stated. Not all countries, however, experience the problem in similar, equally severe ways, and the response to organized crime is not uniform across countries or shared globally. Can the present evidence base be overlooked? Can the significant evidence gaps be by-passed? What is this reaction about?

The thread connecting the various contexts and types of activity of organized crime, beyond the obvious fact that legal restrictions or prohibitions apply, is that they invariably involve the production and supply of goods and services. Without the buying and selling of those goods and services, if the element of trade, and therefore the prospect of a financial gain, is taken away, none of the activity makes sense. Engaging in trade and mobilizing for profit through the trade is a process, and those engaging in it must be prepared—organized—to sustain it. This element of continuity or existence over a period of time, which legal definitions of organized crime typically include, is what differentiates organized crime from the opportunistic crime intended to bring financial gain to a single perpetrator. Time, however, poses important questions about the 'what' and 'how' of the organized activity: recognition of opportunities for viable and profitable business; making decisions about how products will be sourced and made available in the market; deciding how clients will be reached; working out how an advantage over any existing competition will be gained.

These vital practical aspects of the trade are not resolved in a vacuum. The illicit enterprise involved in what is labelled organized crime takes place within a particular economic, social, and cultural environment which both enables and restricts. Knowledge of and familiarity with this environment is indispensable to the illegal entrepreneurs who wish to steer their businesses successfully through it—in fact, it may be a barrier to be overcome precisely by transcending the limitations posed by ethnic or family ties. The idea of the social embeddedness of organized crime captures the necessity for illegal entrepreneurs to possess, maintain, and develop a multitude of links, or 'weak ties' with their milieu and locale. The blurring of the boundaries between licit and illicit activity, and the shortening of the distance between licit and illicit actors, also comes from the mutual recognition of opportunities for financial gain.

Robert Merton, one of the most prominent sociologists of the 20th century, suggested that organized crime and legitimate business were not economically distinguishable. Among criminologists, Merton is remembered as the proponent of anomie theory, which understood an individual's behaviour as the outcome of the balance between the goals and aspirations sanctioned by society and the available means to achieve them. Interestingly, crime appears to fall in the category of innovation, occurring in the absence of legitimate means to achieve the goals and aspirations society sets for people. It is not difficult to see that illicit enterprise is not organized around a value system radically different from that defined by mainstream society. Entrepreneurship, taking up an opportunity, and upwards social mobility are cherished equally by those involved in either the licit or the illicit economy. Those involved in the latter often construe their involvement as being simply a trade and a service that are in fundamental agreement with mainstream values. Equally, the demand for such illicit goods and services is driven by a diverse range of legitimate lifestyle aspirations and demands, such as having a great night out, wearing clothes or accessories that catch the eye, cultural consumption, and so on. These correspond to existing and legitimate markets for such or similar goods and services. In this respect, involvement in the illicit sector, from a trader's perspective, would appear to represent a shortcut, which can be of critical importance for the continuation of their business, or even for survival, in what often are fiercely antagonistic environments and challenging life conditions.

Our final word must rest with the question of waging 'war' with organized crime. Clearly, the activities organized crime involves can and do affect individuals and communities in many harmful ways. It should be equally clear to our readers, however, that countering it requires more than asking straightforward, technical questions about crime control. Illicit enterprise makes sense to the entrepreneurs and others benefiting from it, in so far as it may represent the means by which they attempt to overcome the limitations of their socio-economic positions or to fulfil their personal aspirations. At the same time, illicit enterprise can represent a threat to systemic stability and the established interests of society, locally, nationally, and globally: it opens the possibility for far more players to enter the money-making game in ways that cannot be predicted and controlled. The language and mentality of 'war' very much reflect the fact that genuine social divisions and substantial power differentials forcefully shape the ways in which this conflictual social reality is represented and constructed as an issue. Declaring 'war', however, is no substitute for the creation of a sound institutional design backed up by substantive and extensive knowledge of the various manifestations of organized crime when it comes to effectively addressing the problems posed by it.

References and further reading

Chapter 1: What is organized crime?

Albanese, J. (2015). *Organised Crime* (7th edn). Amsterdam: Elsevier.
Beare, M. (ed.). (2003). *Critical Reflections on Transnational Organised Crime*. Toronto: University of Toronto Press.
Castells, M. (1996). *The Rise of the Network Society*. Oxford: Blackwell Publishers.
Edwards, A., and Gill, P. (eds) (2003). *Transnational Organised Crime*. London: Routledge.
Finckenauer, J. (2005). 'Problems of definition', *Trends in Organised Crime* 8(3), 63–83.
Kleemans, E. (2014). 'Theoretical perspectives on organised crime'. In L. Paoli (ed.), *The Oxford Handbook of Organised Crime* (pp. 32–52). Oxford: OUP.
Levi, M. (2012). 'The organisation of serious crimes for gain'. In M. Maguire, R. Morgan, and R. Reiner (eds), *The Oxford Handbook of Criminology* (5th edn, pp. 595–622). Oxford: OUP.
Reuter, P. (1983). *Disorganised Crime*. Cambridge, MA: MIT Press.
von Lampe, K. (2001). 'Not a process of enlightenment', *Forum on Crime and Society* 1(2), 99–116.

Chapter 2: Organized crime structures around the globe

Italian and Italian-American organized crime
Abadinsky, H. (2013). *Organised Crime*. Wandsworth: Cengage.
Albini, J. (1971). *The American Mafia*. NY: Appleton-Century-Crofts.
Alexander, S. (1988). *The Pizza Connection*. New York: Diane.

Arlacchi, P. (1986). *Mafia Business*. London: Verso.

Catanzaro, R. (1992). *Men of Respect*. New York: The Free Press.

Cressey, D. (1969). *Theft of the Nation*. New York: Harper and Row.

Critchley, D. (2009). *The Origin of Organised Crime in America*. London: Routledge.

Gambetta, D. (1993). *The Sicilian Mafia*. Cambridge, MA: Harvard University Press.

Jacobs, B. (2007). *Mobsters, Unions and Feds*. New York: NYU Press.

Landesco, J. (1968). *Organised Crime in Chicago*. Chicago, IL: University of Chicago Press.

Paoli, L. (2003). *Mafia Brotherhoods*. New York: OUP.

Potter, G. (1994). *Criminal Organisations*. Prospect Heights, IL: Waveland Press.

Savona, E. (2010). 'Infiltration of the public construction industry by Italian organised crime'. In Bullock, K., Clarke, R.V., and Tilley, N. (eds), *Situational Prevention of Organised Crimes* (pp. 130–50). Cullompton: Willan.

Sergi, A., and Lavorgna, A. (2016.) *'Ndrangheta*. London: Palgrave.

US Senate (1951). *Special Committee to Investigate Organized Crime in Interstate Commerce*. New York: Didier.

Varese, F. (2011). *Mafias on the Move*. Princeton, NJ: Princeton University Press.

Woodiwiss, M. (2001). *Organised Power and American Power*. Toronto: University of Toronto Press.

British organized crime

Chesney, K. (1970). *The Victorian Underworld*. London: Purnell.

Dorn, N., Murji, K., and South, N. (1992). *Traffickers*. London: Routledge.

Hobbs, D. (1988). *Doing the Business*. Oxford: Clarendon.

Hobbs, D. (1995). *Bad Business*. Oxford: OUP.

Hobbs, D. (2013). *Lush Life*. Oxford: OUP.

Levi, M. (1981). *The Phantom Capitalists*. Aldershot: Gower.

McIntosh, M. (1975). *The Organisation of Crime*. London: Macmillan.

Morton, J. (2003). *East End Gangland*. London: Time Warner.

Ruggiero, V., and South, N. (1997). 'The late modern city as a Bazaar', *British Journal of Sociology* 48(1), 54–70.

Thomas, D. (2003). *An Underworld at War*. London: Murray.

Russian organized crime

Finckenauer, J., and Waring, E. (1998). *Russian Mafia in America*. Boston, MA: Northeastern University Press.

Galeotti, M. (ed.) (2002). *Russian and Post-Soviet Organised Crime*. Dartmouth: Ashgate.

Gilinskiy, Y., and Kostjukovsky, Y. (2004). 'From thievish artel to criminal corporation'. In C. Fijnaut and L. Paoli (eds), *Organised Crime in Europe* (pp. 191–202). Dordrecht: Springer.

Rawlinson, P. (2010). *From Fear to Fraternity*. London: Pluto.

Siegel, D. (2003). 'The transnational Russian Mafia'. In D. Siegel, H. van de Bunt, and D. Zaitch (eds), *Global Organised Crime* (pp. 51–62). Dordrecht: Kluwer.

Stephenson, S. (2015). *Gangs of Russia*. Ithaca, NY: Cornell University Press.

Varese, F. (2001). *The Russian Mafia*. Oxford: OUP.

Volkov, V. (2002). *Violent Entrepreneurs*. Ithaca, NY: Cornell University Press.

Turkish organized crime

Beşe, E. (2005). 'A sociological analysis of organised crime in Turkey'. Unpublished doctoral thesis. Ankara: Middle-East Technical University.

Bovenkerk, F., and Yeşilgöz, Y. (1998). *De maffia van Turkije*. Amsterdam: Meulenhoff.

Cenzig, M. (2010). 'The globalisation of Turkish organised crime and the policy response'. Unpublished doctoral thesis. Fairfax, VA: George Mason University.

Gingeras, R. (2014). *Heroin, Organised Crime and the Making of Modern Turkey*. Oxford: OUP.

Yesilgöz, Y., and Bovenkerk, F. (2004). 'Urban knights and rebels in the Ottoman Empire'. In C. Fijnaut and L. Paoli (eds), *Organised Crime in Europe* (pp. 203–24). Dordrecht: Springer.

Latin American organized crime

Beittel, J. (2015). *Mexico: Organised Crime and Drug Trafficking Organisations*. Washington, DC: CRS.

Bowden, M. (2001). *Killing Pablo*. New York: Atlantic Monthly Press.

Clawson, P., and Lee, R.W. III (1996). *The Andean Cocaine Industry*. New York: Macmillan.

Decker, S., and Townsend Chapman, M. (2008). *Drug Smugglers on Drug Smuggling*. Philadelphia: Temple University Press.

Dube, A., Dube, O., and García-Ponce, O. (2013). 'Cross-border spillover', *American Political Science Review* 107(3), 397–417.

Grillo, I. (2011). *El Narco*. London: Bloomsbury.

Grayson, G.W. (2014). *The Evolution of Los Zetas in Mexico and Central America*. Carlisle, PA: U.S. Army College.

Lupsha, P. (1981). 'Drug Trafficking', *Journal of International Affairs* 35(1), 95–115.

Rios, V. (2013). 'Why did Mexico become so violent?', *Trends in Organised Crime* 16(2), 138–55.

Thoumi, F. (2003). *Illegal Drugs, Economy and Society in the Andes*. Baltimore, MA: John Hopkins University Press.

Zabludoff, S. (1997). 'Colombian Narcotics Organisations as Business Enterprises', *Transnational Organised Crime* 3(2), 20–49.

Zaitch, D. (2002). *Trafficking Cocaine*. The Hague: Kluwer.

Chinese organized crime

Broadhurst, R. (2013). 'The suppression of black societies in China', *Trends in Organised Crime* 16(1), 95–113.

Chen, A. (2005). 'Secret societies and organised crime in contemporary China', *Modern Asia Studies* 39(1), 77–107.

Chin, K.-L. (1996). *Chinatown Gangs*. New York: OUP.

Chin, K.-L., and Godson, R. (2006). 'Organised crime and the political-criminal nexus in China', *Trends in Organised Crime* 9(3), 5–44.

Chu, Y.K. (2000.) *The Triads as Business*. New York: Routledge.

Lo, T.W. (2010). 'Beyond social capital: triad organised crime in Hong Kong and China', *British Journal of Criminology* 50, 851–72.

Morgan, W.P. (1960). *Triad Societies in Hong Kong*. Hong Kong: Government Printer.

Wang, P. (2017). *The Chinese Mafia*. Oxford: OUP.

Xia, M. (2008). 'Organisational formations of organised crime in China', *Journal of Contemporary China* 17, 1–23.

Zhang, S.X. (2008). *Chinese Human Smuggling Organisations*. Stanford, CA: Stanford University Press.

Japanese organized crime

Adelstein, J. (2010). 'The last Yakuza', *World Policy Journal* August. Available online at: <http://www.worldpolicy.org>.

Hill, P. (2003). *The Japanese Mafia*. Oxford: OUP.

Kaplan, D.E., and Dubro, A. (2003). *Yakuza*. Los Angeles, CA: University of California Press.

Siniawer, E.M. (2012). 'Befitting bedfellows: Yakuza and the state in modern Japan', *Journal of Social History* 45(3), 623–41.

Yokoyama, M. (1999). 'Trends of organised crime by Boryokudan in Japan'. In S. Einstein and M. Amir (eds), *Organised Crime* (pp. 135–54). Chicago, IL: University of Illinois.

Outlaw motorcycle gangs

Barker, T. (2007). *Biker Gangs and Organised Crime*. Cincinnati, OH: Anderson.

Langton, J. (2006). *Fallen Angel*. Mississauga, ON: Wiley.

Lauchs, M., Bain, A., and Bell, P. (2015). *Outlaw Motorcycle Gangs*. London: Palgrave.

Morselli, C. (2009). 'Hells angels in springtime', *Trends in Organised Crime* 12(2), 145–58.

Quinn, J.F. (2001). 'Angels, bandidos, outlaws and pagans', *Deviant Behaviour* 22(4), 379–99.

Thompson, T. (2011). *Outlaws*. London: Hodder & Stoughton.

Wolf, D.R. (1991). *The Rebels*. Toronto: University of Toronto Press.

Chapter 3: The business of organized crime

Drug trafficking

Adler, P. (1985). *Wheeling and Dealing*. New York: Columbia University Press.

Bourgois, P. (1995). 'Workaday world, crack economy', *The Nation* 4 December, 706–11.

Paoli, L., Greenfield, V., and Reuter, P. (2008). *The World Heroin Market*. New York: OUP.

Pearson, G., and Hobbs, D. (2001). *Middle Market Drug Distribution*. London: Home Office.

Reuter, P. (2009). 'Systemic violence in drug markets', *Crime, Law and Social Change*. DOI 10.1007/s10611-009-9197-x.

Reuter, P., and Haaga, J. (1989). *The Organisation of High Level Drug Markets*. Santa Monica, CA: RAND.

Thoumi, F. (2003). *The Numbers' Game*. Available online at: <http://www.tni.org/crime-docs/numbers.pdf>.

UNODC (2016). *World Drug Report, 2016*. Vienna: UNODC.

van Duyne, P.C., and Levi, M. (2005). *Drugs and Money*. London: Routledge.

Migrant smuggling

Antonopoulos, G.A., and Winterdyk, J.A. (2006). 'The smuggling of migrants in Greece', *European Journal of Criminology* 3(4), 439–61.

Di Nicola, A., and Musumeci, G. (2014). *Confessioni di un trafficante di uomini*. Milano: Chiare Lettere.

Içduygu, A., and Toktas, S. (2002). 'How do smuggling and trafficking operate via irregular border crossings in the Middle-East?', *International Migration* 40(6), 25–54.

Koser, K. (2008). 'Why migrant smuggling pays', *International Migration* 46(2), 3–26.

Schloenhardt, A. (1999). 'Organised crime and the business of migrant trafficking', *Crime, Law and Social Change* 32(3), 203–33.

UNODC (2010). *Understanding the Smuggling of Migrants*. Vienna: UNODC.

Zhang, S.X., and Chin, K.-L. (2002). 'Enter the dragon', *Criminology* 40(4), 737–67.

Human trafficking

Goodey, J. (2008). 'Human trafficking', *Criminology and Criminal Justice* 8, 421–42.

Papanicolaou, G. (2008). 'The sex industry, human trafficking and the global prohibition regime', *Trends in Organised Crime* 11, 379–409.

Salt, J., and Stein, J. (1997). 'Migration as a business', *International Migration* 35, 467–93.

Surtees, R. (2008). 'Traffickers and trafficking in Southern and Eastern Europe', *European Journal of Criminology* 5, 39–68.

UNODC (2012). *Global Report on Trafficking in Persons 2012*. Vienna: UNODC.

van Liemt, G. (2004). *Human Trafficking in Europe*. Geneva: ILO.

Weitzer, R. (2015). 'Human trafficking and contemporary slavery', *Annual Review of Sociology* 41, 223–42.

Illegal trade in tobacco

Antonopoulos, G.A., and Hall, A. (2016). 'The financial management of the illicit tobacco trade in the UK', *British Journal of Criminology* 56(4), 709–28.

Hornsby, R., and Hobbs, D. (2007). 'A zone of ambiguity: the political economy of cigarette bootlegging', *British Journal of Criminology* 47, 551–71.

Joossens, L., Merriman, D., Ross, H., and Raw, M. (2009). *How Eliminating the Global Illicit Cigarette Trade Would Increase Tax Revenue and Save Lives*. Paris: IUTLD.

Shen, A., Antonopoulos, G.A., and von Lampe, K. (2010). 'The dragon breathes smoke', *British Journal of Criminology* 50(2), 239–58.

Vander Beken, T., Janssens, J., Verpoest, K., Balcaen, A., and Vander Laenen, F. (2008). 'Crossing geographical, legal and moral boundaries: the Belgian cigarette black market', *Tobacco Control* 17(1), 60–5.

von Lampe, K. (2002). 'The trafficking of untaxed cigarettes in Germany'. In P. van Duyne, K. von Lampe, and N. Passas (eds), *Upperworld and Underworld in Cross-Border Crime* (pp. 141–61). Nijmegen: WLP.

von Lampe, J., and Kurti, M. (2016). 'The illegal cigarette trade in New York City', *Trends in Organised Crime*. DOI: 10.1007/ s12117-016-9291-2.

Counterfeiting

Chaudhry, P.E., and Zimmerman A. (2013). *Protecting Your Intellectual Property Rights*. New York: Springer.

Hall, A., and Antonopoulos, G.A. (2016). *Fake Meds Online*. London: Palgrave.

Interpol (2014). *Against Organised Crime*. Available online at <www. interpol.int>.

Mackenzie, S. (2010). 'Counterfeiting as corporate externality', *Crime, Law and Social Change* 54, 21–38.

OECD (2016). *Trade in Counterfeit and Pirated Goods*. Paris: OECD.

Soudijn, M.R.J., and Zegers, B.C.H (2012). 'Cyber-crime and virtual offender convergence'. *Trends in Organised Crime* 15(2/3), 111–29.

Union des Fabricants (2016). *Counterfeiting and Terrorism*. Paris: UdF.

UNODC (2015). *The Illicit Trafficking in Counterfeit Goods and Transnational Organised Crime*. Vienna: UNODC.

Wall, D.S., and Large, J. (2010). 'Jailhouse frocks', *British Journal of Criminology* 50(6), 1094–116.

Yar, M. (2005). 'A deadly faith in fakes', *Internet Journal of Criminology*. Available online at: <www.internetjournalofcriminology.com>.

Arms trafficking

Bricknell, S. (2012). *Firearm Trafficking and Serious and Organised Crime Gangs*. Canberra: Australian Institute of Criminology.

Europol (2013.) *Serious Organised Crime Threat Assessment*. The Hague: Europol.

Lewis, R. (1998). 'Drugs, war and crime in the post-Soviet Balkans'. In V. Ruggiero, South, and I. Taylor (eds), *The New European Criminology* (pp. 216–29). London: Routledge.

Naylor, R.T. (2002). *Wages of Crime*. Ithaca, NY: Cornell University Press.

Ruggiero, V. (1996). 'War markets', *Social and Legal Studies* 5(1), 5–20.

Schroeder, M., and Lamb, G. (2006). 'The illicit arms trade in Africa', *African Analyst* 1, 69–78.

Small Arms Survey (2013). *Small Arms Survey*. Available online at: <http://www.smallarmssurvey.org/publications/by-type/yearbook/small-arms-survey-2013.html>.

Small Arms Survey (2016). 'The mechanics of small arms trafficking from the U.S.', *Issue Brief* 17, 1–16.

Extortion/protection

Choo, K.R. (2008). 'Organised crime groups in cyberspace', *Trends in Organised Crime* 11(3), 270–95.

Gambetta, D. (1993). *The Sicilian Mafia*. Cambridge, MA: Harvard University Press.

Hobbs, D. (2010). 'Extortion'. In F. Brookman, M. Maguire, Pierpoint, and T. Bennett (eds), *Handbook on Crime* (pp. 726–37). Devon: Willan.

Kelly, R.J., Chin, K.-L., and Fagan, J. (1993). 'The dragon breathes fire', *Crime, Law and Social Change* 19(3), 245–69.

Konrad, K., and Skaperdas, S. (1998). 'Extorion', *Economica* 65, 461–77.

Schelling, T. (1976). 'What is the business of organised crime?'. In F. Ianni,and E. Ruess-Ianni (eds), *The Crime Society* (pp. 69–82). New York: Time-Mirror.

Varese, F. (2001). *The Russian Mafia*. Oxford: OUP.

Volkov, V. (1999). 'Violent entrepreneurship in post-communist Russia', *Europe-Asia Studies* 51(5), 741–54.

von Lampe, K. (2016). *Organised Crime*. Los Angeles, CA: Sage.

Wang, P. (2014). 'Extra-legal protection in China', *British Journal of Criminology* 54(5), 809–30.

Loansharking / illegal money lending

Anderson, A.G. (1979). *The Business of Organised Crime*. Stanford, CA: Hoover.

Birkhead, J.B. (1941). 'Collection tactics of illegal lenders', *Law and Contemporary Problems* (8)1, 78–87.

Ellison, A., Dignan, T., Forster, B., and Whyley, C. (2010). *Interim Evaluation of the National Illegal Money Lending Projects.* London: Policis.

Goldstock, R., and Coenen, D. (1980). 'Controlling the contemporary loanshark', *Cornell Law Review* 65(2), 131–278.

Haller, M., and Alviti, J. (1977). 'Loansharking in American cities', *The American Journal of Legal History* 21(2), 125–56.

Kaplan, L., and Matteis, S. (1968). 'The economics of loansharking', *American Journal of Economics and Sociology* 27(3), 239–52.

Kojouharov, A., and Rusev, A. (2016). 'Sharks in sheep's clothing'. In G.A. Antonopoulos (ed.), *Illegal Entrepreneurship: Organised Crime and Social Control* (pp. 101–21). New York: Springer.

Naylor R.T. (2002). *A Typology of Profit-Driven Crimes.* Ottawa: Statistics Canada.

Scaglione, A. (2014). 'Estimating the size of the loansharking market in Italy', *Global Crime* 15, 77–92.

Silke, A. (2000). 'Drink, drugs, and rock'n'roll', *Studies in Conflict and Terrorism* 23(2), 107–27.

Soudijn, M., and Zhang, S. (2013). 'Taking loan sharking into account', *Trends in Organised Crime* 16, 13–30.

Corporate crime

Braithwaite, J. (1984). *Corporate Crime in the Pharmaceutical Industry.* London: Routledge.

Clinard, M., and Yeager, P. (1980). *Corporate Crime.* New York: Free Press.

Croall, H. (2009). 'White-collar crime, consumers and victimization', *Crime, Law and Social Change* 51, 127–46.

CSD (2015). *Financing of Organised Crime.* Sofia: CSD.

Grabosky, P., and Braithwaite, J. (1987). 'Corporate crime in Australia', *Trends and Issues in Crime and Criminal Justice* 5, 1–4.

Levi, M. (1981). *The Phantom Capitalists.* London: Heinemann.

Passas, N. (2005). 'Lawful but awful', *Journal of Socio-Economics* 34(6), 771–86.

Pearce, F., and Tombs, S. (1998). *Toxic Capitalism.* Aldershot: Dartmouth.

Punch, M. (1996). *Dirty Business.* London: Sage.

Ruggiero, V. (1996). *Organised and Corporate Crime in Europe.* Aldershot: Dartmouth.

Ruggiero, V., and South, N. (2010). 'Green criminology and dirty collar crime', *Critical Criminology* 18, 251–62.

Shover, N., Fox, G., and Mills, M. (1994). 'Long-term consequences of victimisation by white-collar crime', *Justice Quarterly* 11, 75–98.

van Duyne, P.C., and Block, A. (1994). 'Organised cross-Atlantic crime', *Crime, Law and Social Change* 22(2), 127–47.

Money laundering

FATF (2010). *Money Laundering Through Money Remittance and Currency Exchange Providers*. Paris: FATF.

Hot Doc (2014). 'Mona Lisa launders dirty money', *Hot Doc* February, 10–23.

Levi, M. (2013). *Drug Law Enforcement and Financial Investigation Practices*. London: IDPC.

Levi, M., and Reuter, P. (2006). 'Money laundering', *Crime and Justice* 34(1), 289–375.

Naylor, R.T. (2002). *Wages of Crime*. Ithaca, NY. Cornell University Press.

Passas, N. (2005). *Informal Value Transfer Systems and Criminal Activities*. The Hague: WODC.

Reuter, P., and Truman, E. (2004). *Chasing Dirty Money*. Washington, DC: Institute for International Economics.

Soudijn, M., and Reuter, P. (2016). 'Cash and carry', *Crime, Law and Social Change* 66(3), 271–90.

Stothard, M. (2016). 'My brief career as an Indian Ocean tax pirate', *Financial Times* 9–10 April, 11.

van de Bunt, H., and van Dijken, A. (2003). 'Official and informal financial services'. In H. van de Bunt and C. van der Schoot (eds), *Prevention of Organised Crime* (pp. 55–62). The Hague: WODC.

van Duyne, P.C. (1994). 'Money laundering', *Journal of Asset Recovery and Financial Crime* 2(1), 103–42.

van Duyne, P.C., and Levi, M. (2005). *Drugs and Money*. London: Routledge.

Chapter 4: Controlling and preventing organized crime

Andreas, P., and Nadelmann, E.A. (2006). *Policing the Globe*. New York: OUP.

Blakey, G.R. (2006). 'RICO'. *Trends in Organised Crime* 9(4), 8–34.

Bruggeman, W. (2000). *Europol—A European FBI in the Making?* Lecture at Cicero Foundation, Paris, 13–14 April.

Bullock, K., Clarke, R.V., and Tilley, N. (eds) (2010). *Situational Prevention of Organised Crimes*. Cullompton: Willan.

Calderoni, F. (2010). *Organised Crime Legislation in the EU*. Heidelberg: Springer.

Duggan, C. (1989). *Fascism and the Mafia*. New Haven: Yale University Press.

FATF (2012). *International Standards on Combating Money Laundering and the Financing of Terrorism and Proliferation*. Paris: FATF.

Felson, M. (1998). *Crime and Everyday Life* (2nd edn). Thousand Oaks, CA: Pine Forge.

Fijnaut, C., and Jacobs, J. (eds) (1991). *Organised Crime and its Containment*. Deventer: Kluwer.

Harfield, C. (2008). 'The organisation of "organised crime policing" and its international context', *Criminology and Criminal Justice* 8(4), 483–507.

Morselli, C., and Kazemian, L. (2004). 'Scrutinising RICO', *Critical Criminology* 12(3), 351–69.

Naylor, R.T. (2011). 'The international anti-money laundering regime'. In G.A. Antonopoulos, M. Groenhuijsen, J. Harvey, T. Kooijmans, A. Maljevic, and K. von Lampe (eds), *Usual and Unusual Organising Criminals in Europe and Beyond* (pp. 131–50). Apeldoorn: Maklu.

Passas, N. (1999). 'Globalisation, criminogenic asymmetries and economic crime', *European Journal of Law Reform* 1(4), 399–423.

President's Commission (1967). *The Challenge of Crime in a Free Society*. Washington, DC: U.S. Government Printing Office.

Reuter, P. (1995). 'The decline of the American Mafia', *Public Interest* 120, 89–99.

Sheptycki, J.W.E. (2007). 'Police ethnography in the house of serious and organised crime'. In D.J. Smith and A. Henry (eds), *Transformations of Policing* (pp. 51–77). Aldershot: Ashgate.

Spapens, A.C.M., Peters, M., and van Daele, D. (eds). (2015). *Administrative Approaches to Crime*. The Hague: Ministry of Security and Justice.

UN (2004). *UN Convention against Transnational Organised Crime and the Protocols Thereto*. New York: UN.

Woodiwiss, M., and Hobbs, D. (2009). 'Organised evil and the Atlantic alliance', *British Journal of Criminology* 49(1), 106–28.

Chapter 5: Business as usual

Block, A.A., and Chambliss, W.J. (1981). *Organising Crime*. New York: Elsevier.

Edwards, A., and Levi, M. (2008). 'Researching the organisation of serious crimes', *Criminology and Criminal Justice* 8(4), 363–88.

Inciardi, J.A., Block, A.A., and Hallowell, L.A. (1977). *Historical Approaches to Crime*. Beverly Hills, CA: Sage.

Jenkins, P., and Potter, G.W. (1987). 'The politics and mythology of organised crime', *Journal of Criminal Justice* 15(6), 473–84.

Kleemans, E.R., and Van de Bunt, H.G. (2008). 'Organised crime, occupations and opportunity', *Global Crime* 9(3), 185–97.

Merton, R.K. (1968). *Social Theory and Social Structure*. New York: Free Press.

Index

FORENSIC PSYCHOLOGY
A Very Short Introduction
David Canter

Lie detection, offender profiling, jury selection, insanity in the law, predicting the risk of re-offending, the minds of serial killers and many other topics that fill news and fiction are all aspects of the rapidly developing area of scientific psychology broadly known as Forensic Psychology. *Forensic Psychology: A Very Short Introduction* discusses all the aspects of psychology that are relevant to the legal and criminal process as a whole. It includes explanations of criminal behaviour and criminality, including the role of mental disorder in crime, and discusses how forensic psychology contributes to helping investigate the crime and catching the perpetrators.

www.oup.com/vsi

FORENSIC SCIENCE
A Very Short Introduction
Jim Fraser

In this Very Short Introduction, Jim Fraser introduces the concept of forensic science and explains how it is used in the investigation of crime. He begins at the crime scene itself, explaining the principles and processes of crime scene management. He explores how forensic scientists work; from the reconstruction of events to laboratory examinations. He considers the techniques they use, such as fingerprinting, and goes on to highlight the immense impact DNA profiling has had. Providing examples from forensic science cases in the UK, US, and other countries, he considers the techniques and challenges faced around the world.

An admirable alternative to the 'CSI' science fiction juggernaut...Fascinating.

William Darragh, Fortean Times

www.oup.com/vsi

LAW
A Very Short Introduction
Raymond Wacks

Law underlies our society - it protects our rights, imposes duties on each of us, and establishes a framework for the conduct of almost every social, political, and economic activity. The punishment of crime, compensation of the injured, and the enforcement of contracts are merely some of the tasks of a modern legal system. It also strives to achieve justice, promote freedom, and protect our security. This *Very Short Introduction* provides a clear, jargon-free account of modern legal systems, explaining how the law works both in the Western tradition and around the world.

www.oup.com/vsi

GLOBALIZATION
A Very Short Introduction
Manfred Steger

'Globalization' has become one of the defining buzzwords of our time - a term that describes a variety of accelerating economic, political, cultural, ideological, and environmental processes that are rapidly altering our experience of the world. It is by its nature a dynamic topic - and this *Very Short Introduction* has been fully updated for 2009, to include developments in global politics, the impact of terrorism, and environmental issues. Presenting globalization in accessible language as a multifaceted process encompassing global, regional, and local aspects of social life, Manfred B. Steger looks at its causes and effects, examines whether it is a new phenomenon, and explores the question of whether, ultimately, globalization is a good or a bad thing.

www.oup.com/vsi